GW00383945

THE WHIM OF THE WHEEL

Best wishes.

[signature]

17.09.01.

To darling Janey, who changed my life
— then saved it

The wind, one brilliant day, called to my soul with
an odour of jasmine.
'In return for the odour of my jasmine, I'd like all
the odours of your roses.'
I have no roses; all the flowers in my garden are dead.
'Well then, I'll take the withered petals and the
yellow leaves and the waters of the fountain.'
The wind left, and I wept. And I said to myself:
'What have you done with the garden that was
entrusted to you?'

Antonio Machado (1875–1939)
translated by Robert Bly

The love I have in my heart for you
is like the reed in the arms of the breeze.

Son et lumière, Karno, Egypt, 1995

THE WHIM
OF THE WHEEL

The Memoirs of the
Earl of Kimberley

MERTON PRIORY PRESS

First published 2001

Published by
Merton Priory Press Ltd
67 Merthyr Road, Whitchurch
Cardiff CF14 1DD

ISBN 1 898937 45 1

Printed by
Dinfewr Press Ltd
Rawlings Road, Llandybie
Carmarthenshire SA18 3YD

CONTENTS

LIST OF ILLUSTRATIONS

PREFACE

When you have reached the second half of your seventies, it's a particular blessing to have all your marbles in place and to be as acute of mind as you ever were. In my case, that applies even after a devastating stroke which nearly carried me away, mind and all.

Having survived such an experience, life suddenly seemed even more valuable than it did before. I'm reminded of John Mortimer, stuck in a wheelchair as I am, who was asked by some damn fool interviewer what he thought about old age. 'Well', he shot back, 'it's better than the alternative'.

So it seems to me. It was from that healthy perspective that the idea emerged of setting down my own memoir of, I think I may say, a less than ordinary life, lived to the full. When I tried to make a start, it suddenly appeared far less easy than it looked. For the truth is that the human mind, especially when it's reached nearly fourscore, may be very good at vivid recollections, but they tend to be as random as floating autumn leaves and about as orderly as a jam-packed attic.

What I needed was a collaborator, someone who could make sense of it all, and enhance my ability to produce sentences as polished as those of Thomas Hardy on a good day. It was then that serendipity —discovery by luck or chance, if you like—came to the rescue. Nigel Dempster, who nearly thirty years earlier had worked for me as a very young man in my public relations company, John Kimberley Associates, wrote three or four paragraphs in his *Daily Mail* gossip column about my memoirs. A lady in Norfolk who knew me in my palmy young days in that county spotted the item and brought it to the attention of Charles Roberts.

He's a journalist, writer and countryman, who happens to live only a few miles across country from my old family seat of Kimberley Hall, and who had already heard many stories (not all of them true) about my hunting, shooting and socialising days as master of the Kimberley estate.

Charles Roberts wrote to me offering to help write the book and a long association followed (with ne'er a cross word between us), as we brought together the jigsaw of my years. We sat down with a tape recorder and Charles with his shorthand pad. He'd then disappear for a few weeks before coming back for another meeting. To him, I owe great thanks. Gratitude also to my beloved Janey, my sixth countess, for supporting and humouring me in my obsession with telling the world about myself. And appreciation to my gem of a secretary, Pat, who spent hours locating lost photographs, following up leads and taking care of the endless details of copyrights and permissions.

Hailstone House   KIMBERLEY
Cricklade, Wilts.   March 2001

1 The author (right) with his stepbrother Michael at a meet of the Quorn Hunt.

ONE

CHILDHOOD AND SCHOOLDAYS

It was a dark moonless night over wartime London, adding to the claustrophobia of the total blackout blanketing the city. German planes droned in from the east and bombs began to fall, their explosions briefly illuminating the scene. Many died that night. For a youngster of 16, not far away at Eton College, one of those deaths was to have a fateful effect on his life and on the estates of the ancient family of which he now became head. Among the dead was his father, John, third Earl of Kimberley, thus leaving one wilful boy as master of a thousand-year inheritance.

* * *

Seventy-seven is as good an age as any at which to pause and take a long, dispassionate look at what you've done with your life. I can't say I'm entirely proud of my record. According to one kindly soul, it makes that cautionary old eighteenth-century tale, *The Rake's Progress*, look like a parson's parade. But by God, I enjoyed it while it lasted, even if I have to repent at leisure.

It wasn't just the silver spoon for me when an ironical Almighty brought me into the world. Oh no! Only the golden variety was good enough, and I've spent most of my life living up to it—and in the process, spending the family gold of centuries down to very near the last sovereign. I was born heir to an ancient family name which traces back its lineage a thousand years, and at the age of 16 succeeded my father as fourth Earl of Kimberley, sixth Baron Wodehouse and eleventh baronet.

If I care to think about it, in my veins runs the blood of an ancestor knighted by Henry I, and of a celebrated warrior, John Wodehouse, who fought on the Field of Agincourt in 1415. He acquitted himself so valiantly that he attracted the interest of old Sir John Erpingham, Master of the Archers, and of his sovereign, Henry V, who rewarded him by granting to him and to the Wodehouses, for ever, the crest, as well as the arms, motto and supporters which I still

1

2 Father (centre in bowler hat) as master of the Cambridge University Drag Hunt with other members of the club.

bear. These include the right to represent Agincourt on our coat of arms, and to assume the family motto, 'Frappe Fort' (Strike Hard). In my own fashion, though not perhaps in the manner that dashing knight foresaw it, I've upheld that motto every mile of the way.

Nearer our own time, my great-grandfather was a senior figure in Gladstone's Cabinet, and served as Secretary of State for the Colonies, Governor-General of Ireland and ambassador to Moscow. Story has it that Queen Victoria announced to him that he had acquitted himself so well in ministerial office that she wished to elevate him to an earldom. After he had offered his grave thanks for the honour, Victoria asked him:

'And what title will you take, Lord Wodehouse?'

'Agincourt, Ma'am.'

'Oh dear, we don't want to upset the French.'

'Then Kimberley, Ma'am.'

My grandfather, in contrast with the first earl, was content to be no more than a county councillor, though he was no less of a personality. He was small, quick-tempered and tough and, once aroused, would fight anybody, no matter how big they were.

3 Father's first flying lesson, 1910.

In 1905 the council was debating a £10,000 extension to the Shire Hall in Norwich. There was fiery disagreement on the issue between my grandfather and a man called Colonel B.B. Sapwell, whereupon Grandpa first threatened fisticuffs and then challenged the colonel to a duel in Paris. Local and London papers relished the story, with banner headlines proclaiming 'Peer's sensational challenge'. Sir William ffolkes, who as the chairman was much concerned for the dignity of the county council, brought the protagonists together the following weekend at a Norwich hotel, and persuaded them make their peace and shake hands. Which they did. It produced from a local wag the following lines:

> 'I'll shoot you dead', cried Tweedledee,
> 'Let's catch the evening boat'.
> 'No guns', cried Tweedledum, 'for me',
> And shed his little coat.
> With rage their hearts were hot,
> Till peaceful ffolkes cried, 'Don't!'
> 'Well if you think we'd better not',
> They both replied, 'we won't'.

4 Grandfather, grandmother, father and Bob ('Bloody old bitch') on the terrace at Kimberley during the First World War.

Grandfather had a many-faceted personality. He could show great kindness and generosity. He might reasonably be called the first Socialist peer, being a staunch supporter of the National Union of Agricultural Workers. Yet at the same time he was very much the nobleman, with a keen realisation of his blue-blood line. When he died, the local paper caught his image perfectly, one feels, when it said of him:

> There was much of the grand seigneur about him when he felt called upon to exert his dignity. He was intensely proud of his historical heritage, and when referring to his ancestors would talk of the remotest of them as though they were living today and he was in their actual company.

He was also an inveterate ladies' man, with many stories told to prove the point—but so too was my father, from whose genes no doubt comes the irresistible attraction that women have for me.

5 Father and an unidentified woman hunting in Leicestershire.

Though neither father nor grandfather came near to my record of six wives, more brief encounters than Trevor Howard, and even more passionate affairs than I can remember.

More than 15 years after my grandfather's death, I was still paying annuities to a string of ladies in the locality whose favours he had enjoyed. By all accounts his dying words were wholly in keeping with the lifestyle he'd enjoyed. He took in the details of the attractive nurse who was tending him and rumbled 'Take off your clothes'.

I remember him only vaguely, for he died when I was eight. I'm told he saw me when I was taken in as a baby to be 'shown' to him. He looked at me cursorily, turned to my nanny and observed: 'Yes, he looks all right. Take him out!'—rather like a bull being led out of the show-ring at the Royal Show. Which leads me neatly to my favourite story about him. Grandfather loved his land and farms and took a great interest in them.

One day he was going round the Home Farm when he came across his estate steward and the stockman trying to get a bull to mount a cow. The bull showed no enthusiasm. At the moment of grandfather's arrival, the stockman was industriously engaged in thrashing the bull's testicles with a large bunch of stinging nettles.

6 Tout cartoon of Father.

'Why on earth are you doing that?' demanded Grandpapa.

'To encourage 'im, m'Lord', answered the stockman.

A brief consideration of this startling announcement produced the urgent command: 'Whatever happens, don't you ever let her ladyship see you doing that'.

Whether there is any link between that punchline, and the local story that my grandfather sent his wife to her burial on a farm cart, is open to question. She was much loved by the local people, according to the tale, and so shocked were the villagers that they walked silently, one and all, behind the cart to the church, to underline their respect for the countess and their dismay at her last journey.

Grandfather and my father could not have been less alike in looks, though they were much alike in their love of women. Father, it seems, was equally attractive to them. He was tall, dark and handsome, and a total charmer. In 1906 he took on a bet which first required that he should become an MP. So he stood as the Liberal candidate for Mid Norfolk—and won. Stage two was that, as an MP, he could gain access to the clock tower of the Houses of Parliament. Stage three was to lure a certain lady into the clock tower—and there make love to her. Which he did. Game, set and match.

Many years after his death, I was still meeting elderly ladies who told me, with great and nostalgic twinkles in their eyes, 'I knew your father very well'. My father didn't marry until he was 41, and set his sights on my mother Margaret, who was being courted at that time by Lord Dalmeny, as he was then known—the future Lord Rosebery. She'd already been married twice before, a mildly shocking record for a woman back in the 1920s. Her first marriage was to Sir Morgan Crofton, which produced one son, Billy. Her second was to the late James Montagu, by whom she had another son, Michael, whose life was to be a tragically short one. Story has it that after she'd left him, James Montagu was thoroughly vindictive about his ex-wife and once publicly ordered her off his land when she turned up for a hunt meeting.

My father was not in the least put off by her link with Dalmeny and, one day at Hurlingham, before a polo match, invited mother to have lunch with him. She accepted, and they drove off in a gleaming, brand new Rolls Royce. The outcome was that father proposed marriage, and mother accepted. What she didn't know was that this romantic manoeuvre was pure Stephen Potter, a classic case of one-up-manship, for the impressive Rolls belonged to the rival suitor, none other than Lord Dalmeny.

My father died in London during the war, killed by an enemy bomb, and I succeeded to the earldom. At the age of barely 17 (my birthday fell a month after Father's death) I became master of a vast

7 Father with Winston Churchill in the early 1920s.

country seat, Kimberley Hall in Norfolk, with a 5,000-acre estate at Kimberley and on the North Norfolk coast at Bacton, considerable ground rents and property at Falmouth, in Cornwall, and a total income which should have been enough to keep even a playboy belted earl content. But that wasn't to be the story.

By the time I was 30 I'd been married three times—and there were still two more to come before I found my sixth and last wife, my adored Janey, who gave my life, and me, a new beginning. Paying off five countesses didn't come cheap. Nor did years of intensive womanising. Nor taking on the undisputed role in the 1950s and 1960s of London's leading aristocratic playboy. 'The brightest blade in Burkes', the *Daily Express* dubbed me.

Bright the blade certainly was at first. But years of high living, high spending and excessively high alcohol intake took their toll. By the end of the Sixties I was an alcoholic, virtually broke, the Kimberley wealth and property gone, save for some remnants in Cornwall, and at my lowest ebb.

But let's go back to the beginning. I was born on 12 May 1924; Winston Churchill, a great friend of my father's, stood godfather to me. The family link with him stayed close for many years afterwards. The first few years of my life were spent at Thorpe Satchville in Leicestershire, where my mother had her hunting box, otherwise known, curiously, as 'The Cottage', which had eight bedrooms, a nursery wing, servants' quarters, extremely comfortable accommodation for 15 hunters, and quarters, probably not so comfortable, for two grooms and the chauffeur.

All this was quite logical, because mother was fanatical about foxhunting, and was acknowledged in her day as one of the best women riders to hounds in the Quorn and Cottesmore country. She invariably rode side-saddle and always looked stunning in her full habit, whether mounted or on foot.

All who knew her found her great fun, but that didn't mean she was very good at being a mother. She led a very full social life, as did my father, for both had their affairs. Father was very much taken up with his passion for polo. He was reckoned to be the best polo player in the world, and certainly in England.

Earl Mountbatten of Burma wrote a classic book on the sport, under the *nom de plume* of Marco. It contains lots of photographs, most of them showing my father demonstrating the shots. He also wrote the foreword to the book. One of his greatest polo-playing

8 Mother and baby Johnny.

friends, and almost as talented in the sport as my father, was Colonel Vivian Lockett. Years later, when I returned to Kimberley from the war, I'd hoped to start my own polo team, and to persuade the colonel to coach it, but unfortunately the plan never materialised.

Back in the early 1930s, before the monarchy fell, Lockett had gone to Spain to play for King Alphonso XIII. Because he played so well, the king's team won an important match and Alphonso was delighted.

'Colonel, you have done very well for my team and I am very proud', beamed the monarch. 'Now, this evening at dinner I have arranged for a most attractive young lady to be seated opposite you ...'.

'Your Majesty is very kind', replied Lockett. 'But I do have a wife'.

9 Mother riding side-saddle with the Quorn in the early 1930s.

As it happened, the colonel did succumb to the lady's charms—and caught a dose of clap for his trouble. This story came to me from a very reliable source, so I have every reason to believe it is true.

My parents didn't have a lot of time to spend with me when I was a child, and so I suppose I was pretty lonely then. As a boy, I have to confess I didn't like my mother very much, but later, after my father's death, we became very close to each other. I always adored

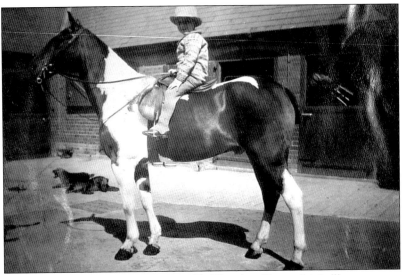

10 Johnny aged five or six on a horse callled Punch at Thorpe Satchville.

my father and was shattered when he died.

When I was about five years old, a great event occurred in my life with the appearance at the Leicestershire hunting box of Gertrude Neat as my nanny. She was a wonderful woman, kind and thoughtful, who loved me and I returned the affection. She taught me to read and write, and also my tables from 2 to 12. So when, aged seven, I went to my first school, Egerton House in Dorset Square, I was way ahead of the other new boys in the Three Rs. I think I was at Egerton for about two years, and was very happy and contented there. I have recollections of us going for walks in Regent's Park, all of us in a carefully chaperoned crocodile, clad in our distinctive dark blue and red colours (an augury, that, as they are the colours of the Brigade of Guards, of which in due course I would become a proud member), and cheerfully whistling 'Marching through Georgia'.

At holiday times, my parents were usually abroad, I don't know where, generally in France, staying in the fashionable resorts. And often separately, I believe. Come Christmas and Easter, my holidays were spent partly at the shooting box, with brief visits to stay with Nursie's mother (for so I now called her) at her little house near Westbury and Longleat. I loved being there because the food was so good. Nursie's father was a schoolteacher in Bristol, and the most marvellous artist and draughtsman, who drew wonderful liners and

11 Lucky, Whiskers and Nursie.

battleships, which fascinated me.

And then there was Westgate-on-Sea in Kent, where Nursie and I stayed in a boarding house. Now whether it is that childhood memory invests things with a rosy glow, and recalls only the more pleasant happenings, I don't know. But Westgate remains for me a child's paradise, in which the sun shone practically every day for weeks on end, and where a day of rain when I couldn't go to the beach was a rarity. There were two beaches, both lovely, proper, sandy beaches, with perfect sand for making really impressive sandcastles. The great thing was to have an iron spade, not a wooden one, because it cut the sand better, though it was a bit dangerous for children.

There I learned to swim. I found out how to catch crabs under the rocks. I also learned to fish from a rowing boat, in which I would go out with a handline and catch dabs and plaice, and sometimes big, edible crabs. Nursie would sit in the stern, I would be in the prow, and the boatman amidships. It was an adventure for me. But as the water was frequently fairly rough and choppy poor Nursie, who was frightened of the sea and couldn't swim, usually felt sick.

But she was a gallant lady, who put up with it all and never complained. Sometimes my father would pay us a visit and I usually managed to persuade him to join me on a fishing trip, though as like as not he suffered from *mal de mer* too. At this time I didn't know

12 Stepbrothers Billy and Michael with Johnny at mother's rented house on Sandwich golf course.

that Norfolk, let alone Kimberley, existed, as my grandfather lived there fairly reclusively. Much as I loved the outdoor life, I was a puny, skinny boy, and it was decided that a spot of the noble art of self-defence would do me a bit of good. So, back at Thorpe Satchville, a boxing professional would come out twice a week to coach me. This was helped along by the arrival of Lord Porchester, 'Porchy' to his friends, who was about a month older than me, and a touch more solid too. We used to box together, under the watchful eye of the pro. I didn't like Porchy one bit, and the feeling was mutual, so it was quite without enthusiasm that I went to stay at his family home, Highclere. My father was a good friend of Porchy's father, Lord Carnarvon, son of the Carnarvon who discovered the tomb of Tutankhamun, and who died, it's said, from the tomb's curse. His body was buried not far away from the house on top of the Downs.

Still, there was one recompense at Highclere, in the shape of Porchy's sister Penelope, with whom I got on famously. Even at that early age I had an appreciative eye for a pretty girl.

I have special cause for remembering being taken to Dunrobin Castle, seat of the Dukes of Sutherland, where in those days the train stopped only if one of the duke's servants waved a red flag! It's a fairytale castle, all minarets and turrets, and one of the most beautiful places I have ever seen in my life, set in a magnificent park overlooking the sea. It was there that I stumbled for the first time on that irrational oddity among grown-ups—superstition. Around the house were many splendid peacocks. One day I found a beautiful tail feather, cut it into the form of a quill pen, and carried it triumphantly inside. There was immediate uproar, with everyone shouting at me at once telling me to take the thing outside because it was seriously bad luck to bring peacock feathers indoors. I got a hell of a rocket for this, which seemed very unfair as it never occurred to me that I was

13 David Charlesworth and Johnny relaxing at Summerfield prep school.

doing anything wrong.

It wasn't this incident though that has left me with such a strong feel for Dunrobin. That lies in the fact that it was there that I killed my first grouse and shot my first stag. I was a natural country sportsman from the start. My first fishing success had come a few years earlier, when I was five. I recall quite clearly staying at Laverstoke Park on the River Test, near Basingstoke, home of Sir Wyndham (later Lord) Portal. He was chairman of Wiggins Teape (who were, and still are, very high class and expensive papermakers) and had several miles of the Test, which was generally agreed to be the finest trout river in England.

I watched all these old buffers casting for trout with flies, and couldn't make out why! My method was a piece of bread on a hook with a float—and I was consistently catching the fish they couldn't. There was a millpond at Laverstoke which in those days was absolutely gin clear. There were hundreds of trout in it, some of them two or three pounds. I was allowed to use my bread and hook method and caught a beauty at just over 3lb, which was eaten by the grown-ups that night for dinner, though I didn't get any of it.

Only about ten years ago I found myself once again at Laverstoke Mill. I stopped the car, got out and went into the mill, only to be told that I couldn't come in without a pass. I told them that the last time

14 Tuck, Johnny and Lucky on the tennis court at Kimberley.

I'd been there was when I was about seven years old and that I would like to look at the mill pond again. It's an odd thing that places recalled from way back are always much bigger in the mind than they are in the later reality. So it was here. As a boy the pond seemed in my eyes to be enormous. Half a century on it was minute. Nor was it gin clear, either, so I didn't see a single trout.

I can't remember when exactly my love of horses began. I have an early recollection of riding a Shetland pony who, like all his kind, was barrel shaped and very uncomfortable for a small boy with short legs, in my case even more so, because I was made to wear toe-cap stirrups. From there I was promoted to a big skewbald cob called Punch, who normally drew the trap. He must have stood a good 15 hands and I remember getting vertigo as I looked down at the ground from the saddle.

Because my father was such a fine polo player, even as a small boy I wanted to be one too. I grew into a good rider, and showed great promise at polo, but later it was as a steeplechase jockey that I was to shine. Even as a boy I had nerve in the sports I played and was never frightened of danger. It was the same later on, when I took a real thrill in the danger of bobsleighing in Switzerland at up to 80 miles an hour. But I confess that, as an active soldier during the Second World War, I was terrified, shit scared. I just didn't like being shot at.

But before those times came, when I was still an eager youngster, my father, being a marvellous shot as well as a brilliant polo player, encouraged me all the way. He encouraged me to exercise so that I could overcome my skinniness and get bigger and stronger. It was he who taught me to shoot, though by then he would never use a gun, having sworn never to do so again. As a young subaltern, serving in the 16th Lancers, he had a terrible spell in the trenches early in the First World War, and was wounded at Mons. Like so many boys of his age, he was thrown into a hell of which they had no comprehension until they got there. He was twice mentioned in despatches, and awarded the MC and the Croce di Guerra. But he returned to England a nervous wreck and was invalided out, when Winston Churchill rescued him and appointed him as his private secretary. At least he survived.

His brother, my uncle Philip, was dumped down a parapet by some fellow officers in a rough bout of horseplay. He broke his spine, was brought back to Kimberley, and died in agony. The official version was that the injury was caused by a wall of sandbags collapsing on him in France. The third brother, my uncle Eddie, who was a brilliant horseman, died early in the Great War at the age of 19.

When I moved on to Eton in September 1937, I was still so small that I was a rowing cox. But I boxed there too, and was pretty good at it, winning several cups which, alas, have disappeared over the years. Again my father encouraged me, and came to Eton when he could to see me box, and to play other sports.

My housemaster had no such feelings about sport. He was a real bastard, and I came to loathe him. He was a misogynist who didn't like men either—all he liked was ancient Greek and Latin. He had a very plummy, patronising voice and dripped superiority. When I was about 15, half way through my time at Eton, he came to me one evening and declared:

'Well, Wodehouse, it's nearly time for you to specialise in a subject. In what have you decided you would like to specialise?'

Without batting an eyelid I said, 'Shorthand, Sir'.

'Shorthand? I've never heard anything so ridiculous from any boy I've ever taught. What a silly boy you are.'

He erupted with anger and made it clear that he thought I was quite barmy. But it seemed logical to me. At that age we had so many lectures at Eton. I spent my entire time writing away, not hearing half of what was being said in the lecture—and not being able to read back what I'd written. I thought that shorthand would be tremendously useful. I could have used it in the army too. But it wasn't to be. To suit him, I had to learn ancient Greek instead, which of course I've used every day ever since!

I fell foul of him on another occasion when, not to put too fine a point on it, I cheated in trials—what they call mock exams these days, I think—faced with a paper on ancient Egyptian history which I knew would be full of dates on who did this and who built that. I knew too it would be misery for me because I never was, then or now, any good at history. Six decades on, I still don't know the kings and queens of England. So, I wrote down on my large wad of blotting paper masses of likely dates. As ill luck would have it, I got caught by the invigilator. At the end of the exam he called me back, and when the other boys had gone he said: 'You know I will have to tell your tutor'.

It was like a sentence of death. It was many hours later, hours endured with a sick ball of worry in the stomach, that the call came demanding my presence in the housemaster's study. When I walked in, he was as black as thunder.

'You have cheated in trials', he snarled. 'You have let me down.

You have let the house down. You can go and see the lower master.' That is, the master who would administer the inevitable punishment, a flogging across a bare backside. This was on a Tuesday evening. The following day was a holiday. So it meant I had to wait nearly two long days for the thrashing. The waiting was worse than the punishment itself. Then there was the follow on, that I would lose my remove. That is, I was going to have to stay in the same form for the next half, instead of moving up with all my mates.

I rang up my father to tell him what I'd done and he was amazingly supportive and reassuring. 'If that's the worst you do in your life, then don't worry about it', he said. He couldn't have been better.

The following day came the ritual. I was marched in by a praeposter to the lower master's room, my trousers were removed and I was put on the block and given seven or eight strokes with the birch, all down one side. It stung of course, but it didn't hurt much, though the marks were there for quite a long time. The humiliation of it was the worst. When it was over and I'd pulled up my trousers, the master put an arm round my shoulder, walked me up and down the room and said:

'Well, now that's done. I'm sorry you've got to lose your remove, but it's not the end of the world'.

This kindness after such an act of mental more than physical brutality was too much for me and I burst into tears. I quickly recovered myself, blew my hooter, and marched out to my friends to put on a convincing act of 'nothing to it, kid's stuff, bugger all', which of course you do. The only thing that I regretted was that I had let my father down. I couldn't care a hoot for having let down that swine of a housemaster. But he, unfortunately, still hadn't finished with me. He knew I was to box for the school, but because I had done some work badly, he kept me in and knowingly stopped me competing. It broke my spirit for a long time. Even now, sixty years later, I still feel bitter towards him.

On another occasion, when I was caught smoking, the rat ordered me as punishment to write out the whole of *Paradise Lost*! I think it took me about three weeks and ruined my handwriting for years afterwards. In fact I don't think it ever recovered.

I hope that bastard is rotting in hell.

Fortunately not all schoolmasters come from the same mould. There's one for whom I have the warmest memories—as well as a certain guilt for not having come up to the heady expectations he had of me. Aged 17, I was sent to a crammer, which happened to be only about 25 miles from Kimberley. I had three special friends, Bing Ironside (later Lord Ironside, in succession to his famous father, Field Marshal Lord Ironside), Bing's girlfriend Candace and my girl, Poppy Honnens. I thought it would be a good idea to pick up a bottle of gin from home, where I'd been spending a weekend, and take it back to share with them at the crammer. So I did, and we settled down together to drink it, though in fact I probably downed most of it. When I got into bed that night, the room began to spin, I felt horribly sick, and didn't know what the hell was happening. I managed to stagger down a passage to the loo, then violently threw up. In my haste, I'd left the door wide open. As I got up, shakily, standing outside watching me was the head of the crammers, a very nice parson named the Revd T.H.T. Evans.

'Where is it, Johnny?', he asked.

I remember, with horrible clarity, looking straight back at him and saying, in a drunken voice:

'Where's what, Sir? I have no idea what you are talking about.'

With that, I staggered back to my bedroom. The next morning I came down to breakfast, and inevitably everybody—about six or seven girls and 18 boys—knew all about it. Breakfast that morning was bangers, and although I was still sick as a parrot, with an awful hangover, I knew I had to eat them and behave as if nothing had happened. Three hours passed before the expected call came to go and see Mr Evans. This is it, I thought, I'm going to get sacked. That put me in a real sweat, because I had only another fortnight to go before I took the exam to go to Cambridge. It was a freezing cold December morning, but Mr Evans chose to speak to me during a walk round the garden. At length he said:

'I don't mind your getting drunk, and I'm not going to throw you out for it. But it may cause you a lot of trouble in your future life if you get drunk on duty.' If only I'd listened to that advice, I might have avoided the sheer hell of alcoholism which I endured in later years. Then this decent, good man made a remark which overwhelms me even now:

'I'd like to think', he said, 'that I've taught the future Prime Minister of England'.

I wish that what he'd said had affected me more. I might have become an MP after the war, rather than a farmer. Who knows? When I think about it, if I'd applied myself and used my abilities to the full, rather than wasting my life as I have done with high jinks and enjoying myself, I could have been Foreign Secretary, as my old friend Lord (Peter) Carrington became. But it was to be 40 years before I took up politics, in my role as a member of the House of Lords.

There comes a time, as the good book says, when one puts away childish things and becomes a man. Perhaps the Revd Mr Evans's words marked my rite of passage. Though in another sense entirely, some months before I arrived at the crammers, the step from one to the other had already taken place. Just as he had foreseen my long-term problems with alcohol, so I had set myself on the path of my consuming passion, the pursuit of women. Up to that point, my sexual experiences had been completely innocent, as with my girl Poppy at the crammers. But when I was in my last half at Eton, I decided that it was time I 'had' my first woman.

I had a dental appointment in London and had worked it so that, between trains, I had just two hours to seek, find and achieve! Before I left, I'd told my chums at Eton what I was about, so there was no going back. That day I was to be seen trudging the pavements in a likely part of the capital, only to discover a great dearth of tarts. In desperation I picked up some awful old bag and we went to her sordid room. Humiliatingly, I wasn't rising to the occasion.

'Am I your first, Ducks?', she asked.

'No, of course not', came my hot young reply. So I left her, so to speak, with my tail between my legs. Naturally, back at Eton I embroidered the tale and told my chums that I'd screwed her, which gave me a great reputation as the first boy in my circle who'd actually got hold of a female. But I wasn't giving up. The next time I went up to London I found a nicer tart—and Operation Virgin was concluded.

That encounter was ironically in my mind when, during the London blackout, I went with my mother to dinner in the flat of an old friend of hers, near Grosvenor House. Being wartime there were no taxis about, and as it was a warm and balmy night we walked together back to the Ritz, where mother was living after her home in South Audley Street was destroyed in a bombing raid. I couldn't help noticing that she was a touch tipsy and was wobbling a little. But she was far from incapable as the following piece of golden advice was to indicate.

'Johnny, my son', she suddenly declared, apropos of nothing,

'Johnny, my son, always be very careful of tarts, you might get a dose of the clap'. She paused, considered, and added: 'Young men go to bed with tarts. They don't go to bed with nice girls. But you want to be careful who the tart is'. It was, no doubt, good advice. But in the wide world of women that was opening up to me, I never did take it. Nor did I ever get the clap!

TWO

A GRENADIER

During my final months at Eton and at the crammers, there had been only one overriding ambition in my mind—to join the Royal Air Force, pilot a Spitfire and play my part in the war. There was another impetus too, a very personal anguish, for during that last Eton term my father was killed by a German bomb in London, when he was working at the War Office for MI5.

The way I heard about it remains as painful to me now as it did at the time. I was at home at Kimberley and coming down the drive from the hall on my motorcycle. Bob Parker, the Kimberley estate agent and a great buddy of my father's (they were at Eton together and of similar age), met me in his old car and asked me where I was going.

'To Norwich.'

'I don't think you should go.'

'Why not?'

'I think your mother should tell you.'

At that moment my mother came down the road in her car and turned in at the lodge. She got out of her car, took my arm, walked me up the drive towards the house—and told me what had happened and how my father had died. I wept with grief, as I do even now, so many years onward, as these words are being set down, for I truly adored him. The anguish was terrible. I still sometimes dream that he is alive, when he talks to me and we are very happy together.

Among people like us it was unusual for sons to get on well with their fathers, though mine was loved by all my chums of my age who knew him. He was marvellous to his stepson Michael, my half-brother. That's the kind of man he was. For most of my school friends, it wasn't that their fathers were unpleasant or nasty—they were just aloof.

My mother, who worshipped my father, handled the situation very well. Theirs had been a very successful marriage, in spite of the affairs which both of them had. But that side of their lives was all kept so tidy—it didn't frighten the horses. Now too the relationship

15 Stepbrother Michael, who was killed in a plane crash.

between her and myself changed. I have to confess that up to then I hadn't been so fond of her, but with Father's death we became much closer.

She was wonderful company, a witty lady who always looked superbly turned out, not least in her riding habit, for she always rode side-saddle.

At Eton I was a member of the Air Training Corps, which I saw as my first step to getting into the RAF. After the painful period following Father's death, I didn't want to stay on any longer than I needed to, and left early at the age of 17.

Following some real work at crammers (and a grateful thought for the clemency of the Revd Mr Evans in not throwing me out) I passed my university entrance exam without any trouble at all, and went on to Cambridge where, in January 1942, I joined the University Air Squadron. That meant that I would be taught to fly and at the end of six months would, with luck, be given a commission in the RAF.

One of my problems as a young lad was that I had suffered hearing difficulties. That was now to come back to haunt me. The Air Force was not very keen on having people flying who had middle ear problems, because of the altitudes one reached.

There'd been various routine medical examinations, but one day the Medical Officer called me in.

'You are slightly deaf, aren't you?', he asked rhetorically.

'Yes, Sir', I replied.

'In which case, you could still get a commission. But you will never fly.'

I was desperately upset, fled back to my digs in Trumpington Lane, lapsed into tears and got drunk. From the age of six, I'd known that I was going to be a flyer in the Air Force. But it was not to be, though it wasn't for want of trying.

When I was sober enough to do so, I rang up Mummy and related my news. She thought a moment and said, quietly: 'I'm glad.' I understood why, because her son and my half-brother, Michael, had died at the age of 21 in a flying accident.

As that summer advanced, mother and I went to stay with the old Duke and Duchess of Sutherland at Sutton Place, near Guildford, owned later by Paul Getty. There was a large house party there, including Lord Robert Cecil, later the sixth Marquess of Salisbury, who had one arm in a sling.

He'd been at a military gathering at Salisbury Plain, where a demonstration had been laid on to illustrate the impact which the machine guns of Spitfires and Hurricanes could achieve on ground targets. In the visitors' stand were officers galore, from full generals down to second lieutenants, who were to discover only too well how efficient those guns could be.

The pilot of a Hurricane confused the visitors' stand with the target, shot up the stand and killed many people. Robert Cecil escaped with a bullet in one arm. Of course the whole thing was hushed up and nothing ever came out.

After the weekend at Sutton Place a group of us went to dinner at the Coconut Grove in Regent Street. It was a good night that went on into the early hours. By 4 a.m. I was thoroughly pissed. It was then that Robert Cecil used his courtly persuasive powers to lead me away from the RAF—and to become a Grenadier. I gave way to his persuasion, and ever since have had absolutely no regrets at all.

Thus I went in as a recruit, not even a guardsman. The form was that you did four months of training and were then promoted to actually being called 'A Guardsman'. I was sent to Caterham, the Guards depot in Surrey, where I found I knew most of the 30 other people in the barrack-room. One of them, years later, became Commander-in-Chief, Rhine Army, General Sir Michael Gow.

Off duty, it was hardly an entertaining place to be. We spent most

of our time polishing brass and boots. In the evenings we'd go down
to a pub, about half a mile away, for a beer. Or we'd head for the
Railway Tavern in Purley, which was thought to be a regular den of
iniquity, though it never was. Not exactly the high life.

There was no transport to get away from the depot, though one of
my fellow recruits had the luxury of a three-wheel Morgan. Every so
often we'd go out in that, and it was a real treat—except on the
occasion he put his foot on the brake too hard and I was thrown
face-first into the windscreen. Bloody painful, but no broken nose!

After two months at Caterham we were allowed a week's leave
before being sent on for another two months to Pirbright. Then we
were really Guardsmen. From there I went to Sandhurst to become an
Officer Cadet, and after six months passed out with a commission.
Sandhurst was an armoured place in those days, awash with tanks.
The teaching was good, and I learned thoroughly to be a tankman.

When I joined my battalion as a second lieutenant, I met the men
in my troop, under Troop Sergeant Pearce. I was younger than them,
but they accepted me because they knew I had come up the hard way.
That was important then. During those war years it had taken me
nearly a year to get that commission.

The day came, in June 1944, when I sailed from Tilbury. Thank
God it wasn't D-Day; it was quite scary enough as it was. I was on
a tiny little landing craft, an American job. It was 'dry' of course. But
I'd had the foresight to take a couple of bottles of Scotch with me, so
I was very popular with the captain.

We were headed for Arramanche in Normandy, though first we had
to steam the whole way round Kent before pushing across the
Channel. By then the British had a bridgehead, so we could beach
without being shot up. The tanks were all waterproofed to go into five
feet of water, though as luck would have it we dropped down into a
depth of only two feet.

Once on dry land, I was given a map, peremptorily told where I
was on it, and instructed to join up with a specific squadron. Bloody
awful tanks they were too. Shermans, with a very small space for five
men. They were called Tommy Cookers, because the defensive
element was so bad that if they were hit, the occupants didn't stand
a chance and were cooked alive!

We went all the way to Hamburg, across France, through Holland
and Belgium, and met plenty of opposition. We had a big battle
outside Caen in Normandy, where we were up against very efficient

16 Johnny with his tank crew, photographed by Guardsman Mason.

German tanks called Tigers. If we hit them with the guns on our tanks, the shells just bounced off. Their gun was the all-conquering 88 mm.

Both sides had a lot of casualties. When the evening fell, we let some of their vehicles with red crosses on them come in to pick up their wounded. They came round the back of our tanks and shot up our lads from the Red Cross vehicles. Typical Jerry. We had been taken as suckers because we were green troops who had not been fighting for long. We never made the same mistake again.

On 1 September 1944 we liberated Brussels—where I arrived in a large Mercedes-Benz. Therein lies a story. We were about ten or twelve miles from the Belgian capital when my squadron leader, who was up ahead of me, called me on the wireless and said:

'My bloody driver's driven my tank into a house and it's immoveable. So I want yours.'

Cursing and fuming, I got out of my tank, and told the driver to go on up the road and report to the squadron leader. At that time the Grenadier group was leading the Guards Armoured Division, followed by the Coldstream Guards. It was the Guards Armoured Division, incidentally, that Goebbels snarlingly called 'Montgomery's Murderers' and 'Churchill's Butchers', which the Guards took as high tribute to their fighting capacity, considering the source of the quotes.

It was one division each of the G.A.D. and the Airborne Force which took on three whole battalions of fanatical Nazis at the Nijmegen Bridge over the River Waal, and thrashed them. Small wonder that we're all so proud of our regiments.

For the moment however, there was I, sitting beside the side of the road, simmering with helpless rage, and watching not only the entire Grenadier group drive past me, but also the whole of the Coldstreams. Suddenly there appeared the very long bonnet of a Mercedes German staff car in camouflage paint, driven by a very characterful Sergeant of Grenadiers. I stepped smartly into the road, pulled rank, held up my hand and he stopped.

'Sergeant, the squadron leader's tank has broken down just round the next corner. Would you please go and mend it and I will take the car.'

If looks could have killed, I would have turned into a pillar of salt. The sergeant was a man of highly individual looks, and the most unguardsman-looking guardsman I've ever seen. He had an enormous, black, droopy moustache, wore great big horn rimmed spectacles and, at better times, a nice smile. As I think about it, I can still feel his eyes boring malevolently into my back as I got into his car and drove off towards Brussels, like Maggie Thatcher used to do to Dennis in *Private Eye*.

I drove past the Coldstream group and through the Grenadier group which my squadron was leading; then put myself in line where I would have been had I still been in my own tank. And so we arrived outside the Royal Palace.

The reaction of the crowds at our arrival was extraordinary, not only welcoming us ecstatically, but offering us everything, including their wives and daughters. The next morning the squadron jeep turned up and was handed over to Captain Lord Carrington and myself, with orders that we stay behind to make contact with all our broken down tanks (we had only six still operational out of nineteen) and stragglers between Brussels and the French border.

Their wirelesses were always switched on, and we could keep in touch with them through our own in the Jeep. When all were repaired and brought back into line, we were to rejoin the squadron.

But during the few days that we were occupied with this operation,

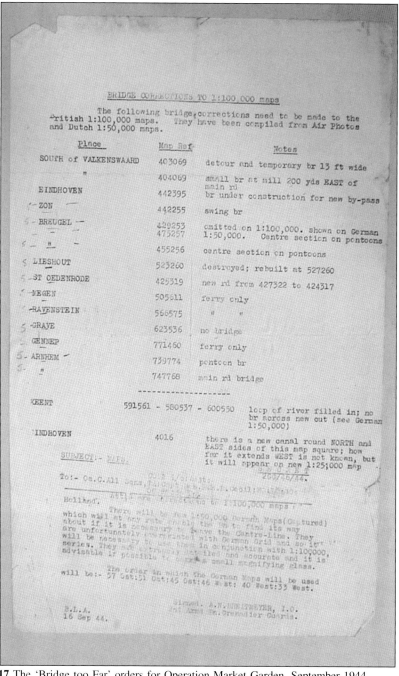

17 The 'Bridge too Far' orders for Operation Market Garden, September 1944.

there was a bright side which I will never forget. We lived in a house of ill-repute! Everything was free: cigarettes, Champagne, food, eggs, women! I was very young, 19 or 20, the sap was rising fast, and they were the most incredible two or three days I've ever had in my life. Peter, I have to say, denies the story that it was a brothel. But he was married, and I wasn't. He had to behave himself, but I had nobody to behave for.

The next fortnight in the north of Belgium, going towards the Dutch border, was a period we were not likely to forget. The Germans knew they were finished, but they still defended their positions with terrific tenacity, and it was a pretty violent dust-up while it lasted.

A great friend of mine, Lieut. Sir Howard Frank Bt, was on my right when his tank was badly shot up. He jumped out with his hands in the air to surrender, and was shot down in cold blood by the Germans. We were not very keen on taking prisoners after that.

Then we reached the nightmare of all places, Nijmegen, where there was a mile-long bridge over the River Waal, which is the bottom half of the Rhine. Once we were over that, we'd be in Germany, a vital fact not lost on its defenders.

It's the one which has erroneously been called 'a bridge too far'. The only reason it was too far, was that half the American parachutists were supposed to have landed on the right or north bank, the German side. But instead they were all on our side of the river—so there wasn't much point in them being there at all.

As a result the Germans mounted a counter-attack from the north side, and in my year and a half of fighting in Europe, I never saw a firework display of such an exhibition of fire power—all, it seemed, being aimed at me!

I lost only two tanks from my troop, which I suppose in the circumstances was not too devastating, although pretty frightening. What was so maddening was that Arnhem, where the British and the 6th Airborne Division were established, was only eight miles away. If we could have reached the bridge at Nijmegen twelve hours earlier than we did, without any doubt 'Operation Market Garden' would have succeeded, countless lives on all sides would have been saved, and the war would have been over by Christmas 1944.

It was all jeopardised by one small mistake—a large mistake, as it turned out to be, of dropping our paras in the wrong place, on the wrong side of the river.

It's interesting to note that this fact, for some extraordinary reason, has never come out in any official history or film of Arnhem, which is pretty iniquitous. So if in any small way this factual report can be of help to future historians, then I am pleased to have the opportunity to make some contribution. And I don't want anybody telling me that I don't know what I'm talking about, because I had under my command not just my troop of four tanks, but a platoon of American paratroops.

On another occasion during that hazardous drive northwards, I remember vividly at one point being holed up in a very difficult spot, held down under enemy gunfire, and needing good advice. It came down the field telephone from one of the best men I've ever known, Major Alex Gregory-Hood, who'd been my squadron leader at Sandhurst. He was a great soldier who was to retire from the Army with the rank of full colonel. He was always turned out impeccably, as a Grenadier should be, and though he was the fairest of officers in his dealings with his subordinates, he could be forgiven during his Sandhurst days for showing a little favouritism for those cadets who were going into the Brigade of Guards. Though in one instance that was severely stretched in my case.

One weekend I committed the most heinous of offences—I went off to London without permission, which was nothing less than AWOL, Absent Without Leave. On the Saturday evening my future first countess, Diana Legh, and I were settled into our chairs in the Bagatelle Restaurant, the smartest in London at that time, where Edmundo Ros played. Then down the steps came Major Gregory-Hood, with the girl who would become his wife.

All I could do was face him out. I walked up to him, greeted him, and asked him if he'd like to share our transport after dinner for an outing to the 400 Club. For years this was the greatest nightclub in the capital, a paradise for those who like that sort of thing. He courteously declined. No reference whatever was made to my being absent without leave.

Monday morning at Sandhurst, there was a drill parade just before lunch. Afterwards Squadron Sergeant-Major Tankard ordered me to report to the squadron leader at 13.45. I had a hurried lunch and was there, at the head of the queue, at twenty to two. I had been there about ten minutes when I was told that the squadron leader would see me last.

So I waited my turn, only to be told when everyone else was gone

that I must come back at 3.30 p.m. So, as ordered, I went back yet
again. I marched in, halted, left turned, banged heels together and
stood rigidly to attention, looking at a point about six inches above
the major's head, as the protocol required. For a time he ignored me,
then:

'You were in London on Saturday night without leave.'

'Sir.' (A Grenadier never replies 'Yes'.)

There was a silence. I lowered my eyes and saw that he was
grinning.

'Don't do it again. Next time it might not be me. If it had been
someone else, you could have lost everything here.'

From that moment onwards I worshipped the ground that man
walked on. On 7 July 1999 I had the sad duty of attending Alex's
funeral at St James's Church, Stivechall, at Coventry, when the
oration was given by my old friend and ex-Grenadier, Lord Carrington.

Looking back, I seem to have been lucky with my senior officers.
Take Lieut.-Col. Sir Napoleon Brinckman Bt DSO, MC, otherwise
known as Colonel Naps. During the war, in the interests of economy,
officers commissioned after a certain date were told not to buy
'evening Blue Patrols', the Grenadiers' evening uniform. This was
easy to enforce because a full set of patrols needed a lot of clothing
coupons, which just weren't available—officially. Which is to say
that, like most rules in life, there were ways of getting round them.

One was via the head porters of certain exclusive London
hotels—the Ritz, Claridge's, the Savoy and the Dorchester. As I've
already mentioned, my mother was living at the Ritz, having been
bombed out of her home in South Audley Street. She had a bedroom,
and an adjoining sitting room furnished with a put-u-up bed. If I had
a night in London, and didn't find a pillow elsewhere, that's where
I slept.

One morning I went downstairs to see George, the head porter.

'Good morning, m'Lord, what can I do for you?'

'I need some clothing coupons, George. I don't know how many,
about 70 to a hundred, I would think.'

'May I ask why, m'Lord?'

'So I can buy my Grenadier evening uniform, Blue Patrols.'

'That seems quite right and proper. May I suggest you come back
this afternoon?'

When I returned, he gave me an envelope containing enough

coupons for all my wants. I went to Kilgour & French, who were not military tailors, but they were the best tailors in London in those days. They are still there in Dover Street, just around the corner from the top of Hay Hill.

I got my uniform, though I don't remember how I managed to get the brass buttons and the right 'stars' to go on the shoulders. Very smart it looked too, buttoned up to the throat and the red stripes running down the trouser legs. Clad in this dashing outfit, I went out on the town that night, met a girl, did the nightclubs with her, and went back to her flat at two in the morning. We spent a few satisfying hours together, then I dressed and at about 8 a.m. left to return to the Ritz. Taxis were like gold dust in wartime London and I couldn't find one, so I had to walk. It's against rules to be out in daytime hours in Blues, so I decided I'd walk on the Kensington Gardens side of the road, where I was less likely to meet someone I knew, as most people walked on the Albert Hall side.

On this occasion, my luck didn't hold. Suddenly I was hailed from the other side of the road by a Scots Guards officer, a captain or a major, I'm not sure which, who summoned me over to him. I marched across, and he demanded to know what I was doing out at 8 o'clock in the morning, dressed in Blues.

'I'm walking home, Sir.'

'Where is home?'

'The Ritz, Sir.'

Well, of course he thought I was taking the piss, though I wasn't.

'But you are still improperly dressed. Don't do it again.'

I was then based at a camp in Yorkshire, to which I returned after the weekend. I found an order awaiting me to report directly to my CO, Colonel Naps.

'I've received some balls-aching report from an officer of the Scots Guards about your being seen in London, in daytime, dressed in Blues.'

'Sir.'

'I have told him to mind his own business. When my officers go out in London in the evening, I expect them to be properly dressed. Continue to do just that. If I hear of you out in khaki, I shall have a row with you. That will be all.'

I thanked him, saluted and marched myself out of the orderly room.

Naps and I became great friends. He was a brilliant infantry soldier, but not so good at commanding an armoured battalion like ours. At Dunkirk he got a DSO and an MC. He was wounded and taken prisoner, but escaped before they had even got him as far as a PoW camp, and managed somehow to get through occupied France and across Spain to Gibraltar, from where he was given a passage back to England.

It was then that he was given command of my battalion. He died in 1985 and was buried, at his wish, in Scotland, for the perfectly logical reason that he had always liked the fishing up there.

But to return to those closing months of the war in Belgium. We used to get 48 hours leave in Brussels every four weeks, which was very welcome because you could get a proper bath, shave and barber at the Eye Club, so called because all Guardsmen have the insignia of the ever-open eye on their battledress shoulders. Incidentally, the ever-open eye was also on our tanks. We could also eat some very good food and chat up—and more, as often as not—pretty girls, of whom there seemed to be a remarkable number.

In the cellars of Brussels, the Germans had left in store the whole of their food for their armies—and the very best for their officers. There was *foie gras* galore, an incredible quantity of eggs for omelettes, plenty of haunches of cured bacon—and buckets of Champagne, though this didn't come courtesy of the Jerries.

It just happened that among our Grenadier officers was Freddie Hennessy, of the Cognac family. The family vineyards in Provence badly needed dressing with blue copper sulphate, which had been unavailable during the war. We did a handsome quid pro quo with Freddie—we sent down there a three-ton ammunition truck loaded with the stuff and he in return saw that we were provided with a load of Champagne! So we had a glut of it, which was very welcome, even if we were drinking it out of tin mugs in a tank.

Our off-duty time wasn't helped by a ghastly organisation which was set up with the acronym of AMGOT, Allied Military Government, which put all the decent clubs and dives off-limits. So on one leave I made friends with a Brussels policeman, asked him to steer me round all the best entertainment joints for the evening, and I would foot the bill for both of us. We had a great time, and plenty to drink.

Too much, clearly, for the next morning I woke up with a thick head, to find myself in a strange bed, and the sun streaming in through a window without any curtains. Then came the next shock.

There on the pillow beside me was a bald head, which was quite horrific to wake up to with a blinding hangover. I was up and out of that bed, and dressed, in seconds, and making for the door.

'Why do you go, Cherie?', enquired a voice from the bed.

'Because your hair has fallen on the floor!'

Presumably she had been a collaborator with the Germans and she'd been subjected by her fellow citizens (none of whom of course had ever dreamt of collaborating with the enemy!) to the due humiliation of having her head shaved. Whatever the cause, it had been a rude shock for me that sunny morning.

It was now about February or March 1945. The war in Europe finished on 8 May. We ended up being billeted in a little schloss near Bonn. The authorities had taken our tanks away so we were once again infantry soldiers. We had been forewarned that we would be going out to the Far East to finish off Japan. I didn't like this at all. I had survived eleven months fighting the Germans and certainly didn't want to go and fight the Japs. So I had to have some reason for not getting posted East.

One day a brainwave struck me. I marched into the adjutant and asked to be seconded to the Parachute Regiment. The next thing was that the Americans dropped a bomb on Hiroshima, which meant the war really was going to be over. Because it was the end of hostilities, the Paras didn't want me, so I never did get round to chucking myself out of an aeroplane, on the end of a puff of silk and webbing, about which in retrospect I'm really quite relieved.

At the end of August 1945 I was demobbed, and returned to my estate at Kimberley in Norfolk, where I became a farmer and was soon to bring back my first countess in what was to prove a brief and utterly disastrous marriage.

But there was one wartime link which, in terms of name at least, connected in a sense to Kimberley. It concerns that contemptible little man, P.G. Wodehouse, creator of the world of Bertie Wooster, Jeeves and the Empress of Blandings. It all started when, as a youngster, I was reading a P.G. Wodehouse book. I asked my father if he was a cousin of ours.

'Yes, unfortunately so', he replied.

Then he told me how, during the First World War, Wodehouse went off to America to avoid being called up in the British Army.

'It was because he didn't want to fight. But he could have worked in a munitions factory, doing something useful for his country, if he didn't want to join the Army.' As we talked, Father's face went dark with anger. 'I hope you never meet him', he said.

There was of course worse to come in the Second World War, though I don't know whether my father lived to know of it, for he died in the same year, 1941, that P.G. Wodehouse began to make broadcasts for the Germans from Berlin. Our view of him was certainly confirmed only recently (September 1999) when previously classified MI5 documents were released, which called into question the widely held image of Wodehouse as a vain but harmless fool.

After the war he claimed that he had merely been a 'silly ass' and 'made a hideous mistake', as if he were a character from one of his own novels. But archives from the German embassy in Paris make it abundantly clear that his naivety and innocence were a sham, and that in fact he was working in a lucrative job for Hitler's propaganda chief, Josef Goebbels.

Everyone seems to have forgotten and forgiven what he did in two world wars, even to the extent of Britain giving him a knight-hood—of course, it was under the Wilson government—which he lived to enjoy only 45 days before he died in 1975. I haven't forgotten or forgiven him, and I never will. That what he did has been generally forgotten says something about this country.

In some useless biographical dictionary, not the proper *Who's Who*, I had been set down as his cousin. I rang them up. 'Am I like bloody hell his cousin', I told them. 'Unfortunately, on paper at least, he is mine. But I'm assuredly not his. So will you kindly obliterate that entry next year.' And they did.

THREE

KIMBERLEY

Kimberley. A vast, corner-towered mansion set on a ridge a couple of miles from the small market town of Wymondham, in mid Norfolk. It was built by my ancestor, Sir John Wodehouse, in 1712. Previous family houses had existed, all within a mile of the Kimberley Hall site. One was in Norman times, but only the moat and a few low walls remain of it.

There was another in Elizabethan times, known as Wodehouse Towers, which has entirely disappeared. The true story of its fate remains a mystery—some say it burned down; others claim it was demolished.

The present hall sits within its park and estate, and on the garden side looks down from its eminence onto 'the Lake and Serpentine River', as noted by the great Norfolk antiquary Blomefield towards the end of the eighteenth century, and on to gardens which were created by Capability Brown, no less.

There is no connection, except a very tenuous one, with the Kimberley Diamonds, though when in the late 1950s I went to America, every newspaper and gossip columnist assumed that I was loaded with the things and thus fabulously rich. The actual link is almost an honorary one. My great-grandfather, the first earl, was Secretary of State for the Colonies, and the diamond town in South Africa was named after him. Simple as that.

For me as a boy there were riches aplenty, of a different kind, within the park, woods, fields and waters of Kimberley Hall, all of which were revealed to me by my father. Like so many Wodehouses through the ages, both he and I were christened John, but he became Jack, while I from the start was Johnny.

He didn't actually farm the estate; his agent, Bob Parker, took care of all that. But he was a great naturalist. He taught me all I knew about butterflies, birds and flowers. He loved trees and was quite a good artist in crayon and water colours. Like my great-grandfather, another John, he was an early conservationist. Though he left the farming to his agent, he was still always looking over Bob's shoulder to see that wildlife was properly looked after. This really was the

18 Kimberley Hall, Norfolk, from a drawing by J.P. Neale (1820).

beginning of my love for the estate, of which I knew every square inch.

That old affection was rekindled when I returned, following my demob, to a party arranged by the estate tenants to welcome me back and celebrate my coming-of-age four months earlier. They gave me a beautiful, inscribed gold cigarette case. A cutting from the local morning newspaper, the *Eastern Daily Press*, dated 1 September 1945, records that I said to them: 'I cannot thank you enough. I have always been happy here amongst you all and I hope we have a lot more good times ahead'.

Well, there were at least a few good years to come for the estate, though they'd be laced with bitter gall for me.

During the war the hall was taken over by the government for military use, and latterly as a PoW camp. But I couldn't have dreamed of the horrendous mess it would be in. It was in a terrible state. I contacted my solicitor and told him to get on to the Ministry of Works. They decided they would pay some recompense, but definitely no more than £10,000, which was a small figure even then for the damage that had been done.

The house needed a new roof, every single window frame had to be taken out, reglazed and painted. The roof problem was that soldiers had wandered around up there, God knows what for, in their nailed boots, puncturing the lead sheeting so that the place leaked like a sieve. The old lead was sold off, but replacing it with the same materials would have been hugely expensive. So we came up with an idea, which proved both efficient and waterproof.

We replaced the lead by layering the roof in three-quarter-inch thick tarmac! It was done, over a period of several weeks, by the asphalt company Limmer & Trinidad, who had to haul up every pound of the stuff in a procession of buckets strung on a pulley.

Internally the house was worse, if anything. The beautiful mahogany doors of the library, which were works of art in themselves, had been used by the soldiers as dart boards, and were riddled with holes. The only thing that could be done was to find some really good mahogany veneer, but one could never get rid of the holes.

The ministry's decision was a real kick in the balls. If I hadn't had my own estate carpenters, builders and plasters, I would not have been able to do it. From the start I was engaged in the work myself. I'd learned to be a painter and carpenter at school—I even won a carpentry prize.

I worked with the men and I enjoyed it. They still called me 'm'Lord', but I knew them all by their Christian names and they had known me since I was a little boy, and mighty fine men they were. I learned how to lay bricks too. I could lay more bricks to the hour than a union bricklayer, if I had a man to keep me supplied with mortar and bricks!

I virtually rebuilt the gardener's cottage myself, and was my own architect into the bargain. I knew what I wanted so it really wasn't very difficult. In fact the only real difficulty, at that time, was getting the bricks. Even in 1952 they were, like everything else, still in short supply in the lean, ration-book years following the war.

It took several years to get the house back to rights. During that time I lived in the cottage, which I was to share with my second wife, Carmel. My first countess, Diana, didn't like the countryside and rarely came to Kimberley.

By the time the job really was finished, I had spent twice the £10,000 restoration grant. Yet worse was to come: a demand for death duties on my father's estate, who had still been paying off duties following his own father's death. That meant that I inherited what would be known in today's terms as a 'double whammy'.

This enraged me then and still does. Father was wearing the King's uniform when he was killed by that German bomb in London in

1941, and if that is not active service, I don't know what is. Given the circumstances of his death, surely death duties should have been waived. But that is how grasping government taxation works.

In those first months back in civilian life, and faced with the immense task of getting Kimberley back on its feet, there was also another thought in my mind—of marriage. Back at Sandhurst, I had met at some function or other Diana Evelyn Legh, daughter of Lieut.-Col. Sir Piers (Joey) Legh, Master of the Royal Household, who lived with her parents in grace and favour houses in St James's Palace and Windsor Castle.

While I was still a cadet, I ran into her again at a dinner party in London, and during my active service years she used to write to me. While I was still in uniform our paths crossed again, and my mother was very keen that we should make a match of it. She and Sir Piers had been, shall I say, very close friends, which might have had something to do with it.

But I was so recently back from fighting a war, still a young 21, and not really ready for commitment. Truly my heart wasn't in it—especially as there was another girl in my life whom I was mad about. Perhaps I should never have given way to pressure. But I did, and Diana and I became engaged.

One of my last jobs in the Army, in company with a friend in my battalion named Peter Whitley, was to oversee the clearing up of a camp in Yorkshire, before its handing over to the Royal Army Ordnance Corps. A Corps officer arrived and that evening, we had dinner with him and talked. Unexpectedly he said:

'Would you like to know about the future?'

He was, it appeared, a psychic. We were to make a secret wish, while he concentrated upon us, one by one. In my mind I said:

'I wish to marry another girl, not the one who is due to become my wife.' After a pause, he said:

'You will not get your wish.'

Then he turned to Peter, who told me later what he had wished—that he would not be wounded. Most fellows would have said 'not be killed'. But Peter specifically said in his mind 'not be wounded'. Again a pause:

'You will get half your wish.'

This odd reply came to pass, for soon afterwards Peter managed to get his left knee inside the guard that was protecting a 75 mm gun. It recoiled and smashed his kneecap to smithereens. He hadn't been

19 Johnny with Diana Legh, his first fiancée, at Ciro's Restaurant, London, 1943.

wounded. It was an accident. The prophecy had come true.

On 27 October 1945 I walked down the aisle of St George's Chapel, Windsor, to await my bride. I was attended by my best man, Brig. Alan Breitmeyer, another fellow Grenadiers officer. He was a brilliant soldier and a Wykehamist (all Wykehamists make good soldiers, for some reason) who joined the Army on the same day as I did.

As we walked to our seats I saw, in a pew on my left, the girl I loved and had really wanted to marry, and I thought:

'You are marrying the wrong one. Even now it's not too late.'

I knew, surely, that I was doing the wrong thing. But the ceremony went ahead, to be followed by a grand reception in the royal apartments, with the King, Queen and the Princesses all present. The King, who like me was dressed in Grenadier uniform, proposed our health, and I danced with the Queen, the present Queen Mother, who danced superbly.

It was a handsome and fashionable gathering of about a hundred people, mostly of my parents' vintage. My mother, who always wore black, looked tremendously chic. Adding to the glitter were personalities like Emerald Lady Cunard, Princess Romanovska Pavloska, and Prince Ali Khan.

20 Wedding of Johnny and Diana, 1945. Left to right: Margaret, Countess of Kimberley (Johnny's mother), Princess Elizabeth, King George VI, bride and groom with bridesmaid (daughter of Lord and Lady Grenfell), Queen Elizabeth, Alan Breitmayer (best man), Princess Margaret, Sir Piers and Lady Legh (bride's parents).

We left the next day for a honeymoon in Ireland, first at the Dunraven Arms in Limerick and then to Dublin. From that first interlude it was clear that the marriage had been a ghastly error. We just didn't relate to each other. A classic case of incompatibility.

At the Dunraven Arms, to escape my inner turmoil, I took refuge in practical matters—like tackling the ancient pub's riot of mice in the bedrooms. I went to a local shop, bought a dozen mousetraps and set them in every corner. By the end of our stay I'd caught about nine mice, which was at least some kind of achievement.

As I was quickly to discover, Diana just wasn't a country girl, had no interest in country life and didn't fit into it; didn't like shooting and used to sit with her fingers in her ears. She was happiest in the royal ambience of St James's and Windsor. One sighs heavily to read a yellowing newspaper cutting recording my arrival with my new wife at Kimberley in December 1945, the reception for 300 tenants and friends which followed, and the presentation to us of a silver salver, a cheque and an illuminated book containing the names of the subscribers.

21 The newlyweds leaving St George's Chapel, Windsor Castle, through a guard of honour of Grenadier Guards.

But it is my words to the gathering which drive a dagger into the heart: 'I hope it will be possible to make this an annual event on this date for the children on the estate.' Only fifteen years later that great estate and its close community were gone for ever.

I had set out on the premise that everything with Diana would, after all, be all right. Just as I had set out with the highest intentions for Kimberley, restoring the house, farming my land, and representing my people as the Wodehouses had done for generations.

By spring 1946 I had already successfully campaigned for the Wymondham Division seat on Norfolk County Council, having assured the electors that 'I bring to the work … a tradition that persuades me to devote a large part of my time and ability to public service'. I meant it at the time. But one term on the county council, with all its frustrations and lack of vision, was enough to make me comatose with boredom, and I didn't seek re-election.

So for the time being I had to make the most of my situation and fill in my time as best I could. One morning, a few days before Christmas 1947, I called in for a drink at a rather special club on the Chelsea Embankment called the Garden Corner. It was run by two ex-RAF wing commanders, Bill Wetton (who made a great success of a window cleaning business in London) and Michael Pressland, who together owned two planes, a Percival Vega Gull, and a Dragon Rapide.

'Would you like to go to Zurich next weekend', asked Bill. My first reaction was to say no, but when I realised that the plan was to go on to St Moritz, I changed my mind, and joined a party of seven or eight in the Rapide.

The original idea was to land at Le Touquet, then follow the railway line all the way to Zurich through Basle. But when we reached Le Touquet the weather was so appalling that we couldn't go on. In the group was Billy Rees-Davies, later an MP and a great friend of mine, and together we left the landing field and headed for what was left of the town—it was virtually flattened in the war and of course reconstruction hadn't yet begun.

It was freezing cold, pissing with rain and blowing a gale, and we took refuge in a café with the grandiose name of Harry's Bar & Grill. Four times we went back to the airport and got the plane into the air, and four times were forced by the weather conditions to land again after just one circuit.

Billy and I abandoned the rest of the party and caught a train to Paris, sitting upright right through the night in a very cold and comfortless carriage. At last we arrived—but with the small problem of having hardly any money, as one was allowed at that time to take only £5 abroad. Somehow we managed, though I've no idea how we paid for things.

We took another train from Paris to Basle and from there went on to St Moritz, where we arrived on Boxing Day—the original aim was to be there by Christmas Eve. We went straight to the Palace Hotel where I knew the owner, Tony Badrutt—he, the Palace and St Moritz would in the coming few years play a central role in what was one of the happiest and most exciting periods of my life, when I revelled in the dangers of bobsleighing and in being king of the Cresta Run.

For the princely sum of £1 a night, Tony gave us two minute rooms in the clocktower of the hotel, which were accessible only by ladder! Not too good if you were trying to seduce a young lady and get her into your bed for the night. Still, one could always go back to her place. Which is exactly what happened in a short but wonderful affair with a stunningly beautiful American figure skater. But that story belongs to the next chapter.

Just once I took Diana to Switzerland, in January 1946. We stayed in Davos and took a train to St Moritz to have a look at the town. There for the first time I saw the bobsleigh run, liked what I saw and knew I must have a crack at it. It was in that spring that Diana sailed to America with her mother in the *Queen Mary*, as our non-marriage continued to desiccate on the bough.

It was around this time that, together with an old school friend, Lord Loch, who I had known at Summerfield prep and later served with in the Grenadiers, I tested my entrepreneurial skills. I met him one day, probably in 1947, and he asked whether I would like to buy some vintage whisky in unmarked bottles (which probably meant they had fallen off the back of a lorry) at a very cheap price. I said 'Yes'. I had a Polish friend who was married to a beautiful Spanish countess named Helena Segusta. He had a Rolls Royce station wagon and an entrée to all the nightclubs in London because he knew the owners. He asked whether I knew that if you mixed one third of a bottle of sherry with two thirds of a bottle of Scotch, you could flog it as brandy at clubs, where most people tended to drink brandy with ginger ale or soda water. What we lacked was a place to do the bottling: we needed somewhere you could park a car not far from the front door. Luckily I had the key to a suitable property in Mayfair where we carried out the bottling and stuck on a smart label with Contessa Helena Segusta Brandy printed on it. Her husband provided the transport and as a result of our little enterprise a suitable profit was made. We flogged the 'brandy' for well over twice the initial outlay and I kept a hundred bottles of the Scotch for myself. But that was the end of my bootlegging days!

Back home at Kimberley I had a flying visit one weekend from an old friend, Dr Matthew Banks, whom I'd got to know during the war when I borrowed his car—and unfortunately went off with his doctor's bag with all his instruments in it. We became great pals after that, and he used to fly down frequently to Norfolk in his Auster light plane.

It was through him that I learned to fly. There were two joysticks, and I sat beside him in the plane for hours and hours, picking up the basics of flying. I never did any extensive flying, but just local journeys, jogging along at about 100 m.p.h.

In 1948, the year that my marriage to Diana formally came to an end, I acquired a Healey car, which was both expensive and fast. I can't remember, but it could well have been a celebration of my freedom! Anyway, it cost a steep £3,000, and had a top speed of 125–130 m.p.h. Knowing that the Auster's top speed was only about 110, I challenged Matty to a race to Newmarket.

ʹ I set off for Wymondham and then, once on the A11, let my Healey rip and settled down at 100 m.p.h. Up aloft, Matty had a headwind. On the ground, we didn't. So he was never doing more than 90. There was very little traffic in those days, and the A11 was a very fast road. Enough to say that the Healey finished in New-market a clear first in front of the Auster. We celebrated our contest with a visit to the racecourse—and the backing of half a dozen losers.

On that particular weekend when Matty planed in unexpectedly, he announced that on the following day he intended to fly to the Isle of Wight to stay with Pat Aitken, widow of Captain Peter Aitken, Lord Beaverbrook's son, who the year before had drowned when he fell overboard, drunk, from a yacht off Sweden. Would I like to come with him? I certainly would, as I'd seen photographs of Pat's strikingly beautiful sister Carmel Maguire, and was determined to meet her.

Then, as now, attraction in women is always visual for me! When the looks are right, I can't resist.

Pat lived in a fascinating house near Freshwater, which was made of wood and looked like a boat. It was rather like being on a boat inside, too, looking out onto the sea. She was quite attractive and, well, as I never wasted much time, we ended up in the hay together. She fell in love with me but, though I was very fond of her, I couldn't return her feelings.

Then Carmel arrived on the scene. We met, were immediately attracted, I swept her away and we had a whirlwind romance. Alas I didn't know then about her filthy temper, or I might never have made the mistake (and they say lightning never strikes twice) of later making her my second countess.

Diana and I had been married, on paper, for six months when I was in London for a dental appointment, having driven there in a second-hand American car which I had bought. The thing broke down on me and I thought to myself: 'I've put up with this too long. I'm going to the Bag of Nails'. The Bag of Nails, for the uninitiated, was a seamy club notorious as an expensive pick-up joint.

So there I went, met a lovely blonde called Dorothy, and had a marvellous night of love-making with her. 'You really are a fool K—just pull your finger out!', I told myself. So soon afterwards I was back in London and, having left Diana at St James's Palace, headed for the Bag of Nails, found Dorothy again and worked out my tensions with her willing help.

It was however, rather expensive at the Nails. But Dorothy had been the catalyst that I needed. She made me realise what an odd life I'd been leading, 21 years old and caught for seven months in a disastrous marriage that was never going to get any better.

So I decided to do something about it and the answer was simple—to lay every girl I could lay my hands on, and there were plenty about. From my teenage years I'd had a very strong sex drive. I thought it was normal, but looking back on it, mine must have been fairly potent—and was to remain that way for several decades to come, with inevitably a reputation to match.

Among the Norfolk huntin' and shootin' crowd, everyone knew everyone else, and very possibly everything about them. So when in the 1950s Sir Thomas Devitt, a jaunty baronet with an acute eye and an unstoppable sense of humour, set about penning an epic doggerel poem (printed in full on pages 194–6) about these personages, I was fair game:

> Lord Kimberley, another guest,
> Can wield his gun among the best;
> But you must get him first, 'tis said,
> To leave his warm connubial bed;
> For after alcoholic soaks,
> And super-energetic pokes,
> Suffering from *mal-de-tête*,
> Lord Kimberley is sometimes late

In a way my marriage to Diana was a kind of insurance—while I was married to her I couldn't be married to anyone else. In my heart of hearts, of course, I knew this was nonsense, and couldn't go on indefinitely. One year on from the wedding, I left Diana in London with her mother and father. I needed to discuss the matter with Diana's half-brother, Freddie Shaughnessy.

I already knew Freddie well from the war, when he was a fellow Grenadier officer with me in Brussels. During one of our 48-hour leaves, as we were all setting off to seek entertainment, I asked him where he was going. He replied disarmingly: 'I'm going to a brothel, and when I've done that I'm going on to enjoy the opera'. Though later his speciality would not be opera grand or buffo, but soap, for he was to write the hugely successful television series, *Upstairs Downstairs*.

When Freddie had heard what I had to say about the marriage problem, he straightaway laid the facts before Sir Piers Legh. The result was that Sir Piers and I got together, and it was agreed that a separation was inevitable. In his role as Master of the Royal Household, however, he made it clear that in such circumstances, any links for me with the Royal Family and the Court, including attendance in the Royal Enclosure at Ascot, were strictly forbidden.

With the formal separation signed and sealed, I had the good fortune to meet up again with a girl named Nancy Hunter Patterson, whom I'd seen dancing on my first skiing trip to Switzerland in 1945. I spotted her again at Ascot the following year, somehow got introduced, and took a shine to her.

She was a very athletic looking girl, who skied remarkably well, and also happened to play the piano beautifully, something which always pleases me in a woman. I got her to come down and stay in the cottage at Kimberley. She was fun, but a bit of a nutter—which is how I came to break the four-minute mile, being pursued by her with a carving knife!

I grew out of her fairly quickly, though God, our affair was fun while it lasted. When it came to its end, she used to go round Mayfair looking for my car, wherever it was parked. It was quite a smart Jag, and she would write messages in lipstick all over the windscreen, which was mildly tedious. One day I was in a taxi, returning to where I'd left the car, and caught her in the act. I told the cabbie to stop, picked her up and took her to her flat in Cornwall Gardens in Kensington. I paid the taxi driver and asked him not to move.

What I didn't realise was that, in the instant my back was turned, she slipped him another fiver and told him to get lost. She unlocked the door of her flat and I agreed to come in with her. No sooner was I inside the hall than she slammed the door shut behind me to prevent me leaving, hung on to me frantically like a drowning woman, and said she'd never let me leave her.

Somehow I freed myself, pulled open the front door, got myself outside and slammed the door behind me. An instant later it opened again—and there was this crazy woman with a raised carving knife in her hand, intent on sinking its blade into my anatomy. With no concern for dignity, I took to my heels.

It was a hot summer's afternoon, and I ran all the way to the top of Sloane Street, not even looking to see if she was still on my tail. At long last I got a taxi, pulled open the door, hurled myself in and gasped: 'Just drive'. Blowing more than a bit, for I wasn't too fit then, I directed the cab to my mother's house where I could recover.

Nancy continued to pursue me, though in a more benign form, for years afterwards, with the pestering renewed in earnest when in the 1970s I was regularly attending the House of Lords. The doormen were very understanding and tactful and, with their polished technique in these matters, gently got rid of her. Even then, letters would arrive on my birthday, telling me how much she still loved me.

I didn't see Diana throughout the remaining two years of our marriage, which ended with divorce in 1948, when I tried to make the exit as painless as possible for her. Though the real fault was not mine, I behaved like an officer and a gentleman and gave her grounds for divorce. Though there too, lies a story.

The grounds were prepared, if that is the word, between myself, my lawyer and a private detective. The whole thing was not pleasant. Not initially, anyhow. I received a phone call from a woman who was a professional co-respondent, and arranged to meet her in one of those shabby, anonymous hotels in Regent Street, just above Piccadilly Circus.

'How shall I know you?', I asked.

'I will be wearing a yellow dress, hat and shoes.'

I walked in at the appointed hour, picked out the vision in yellow, and off we went to the Grosvenor Hotel at Victoria Station. She was, I learned, a doubly professional lady, being a solicitor's secretary, as well as a retained co-respondent, and had also been a Swedish gymnast. An element of the latter I was to discover in due course.

At the Grosvenor we checked into a small, freezingly cold and cheerless room containing a single bed and an armchair. I ordered some food and drink to be sent up for her, before telling her that I was now going out to dinner and would be back later. I met Carmel at the 400 Club, where we dined together before I returned to the Grosvenor.

I went into the bedroom where the gymnast-cum-secretary had shed her yellow wrappings and was tucked up in bed. I sat down in the armchair, but soon decided I couldn't sit there all night, because it was so bitterly cold. There was but one thing to do. I undressed, slid into the bed and pushed the woman over a bit. The next thing I knew, I was being athletically raped. It was rather exciting. Later, with due professionalism, she gave the required evidence, and I was divorced.

There is a footnote to this period, poignant and ironical by turns. About six years ago the girlfriend I had wanted to marry all those years before was going through some letters in her attic, when she came across one that I had written to her in July 1944, in pencil, declaring undying love for her. Suddenly to find a letter like that, written more than 50 years ago, is a bit staggering. She got in touch and suggested that we should have a nostalgic lunch together. Janey, my last and adored countess, said that I should go. But I never have, yet I'd love to see her again, half a century on.

FOUR

ST MORITZ

In the decades following the Second World War, just as it had been after 1918, St Moritz was a wonderful place to be: lush, smart, fashionable, full of beautiful people, a magnet to the rich and famous, a marvellous playground, the glossiest of social life. And, oh yes, a paradise for philanderers and affairs. The hub of it all, without doubt, was the Palace Hotel. For me both town and hotel were irresistible, drawing me back time after time. Even to get married.

How good to note, more than half a century on from my first visit, that St Moritz is again pre-eminent, and once more a magnet to the world's top-drawer people. And at the heart of it, the old Palace lives on—though now under the amazingly unwieldy title of the Badrutts Rosewood Palace Hotel!

I first went skiing in Switzerland in 1945 with some friends from Norfolk, all two or three years older than me, who already had some skiing experience from before the war. My first attempts on the nursery slopes had me cart-wheeling ten times over. After lunch, fortified by a little Swiss brandy, I tried again, with just a little more success.

Then someone suggested a merry jaunt—to go to the top of the mountain and ski the twelve miles to Klosters. And that's how I really learned to ski, through falling over God knows how many times, doggedly getting up and going on each time, and having the terrific satisfaction of getting down to the bottom of the mountain, and in one piece too.

A few days later we decided to go to St Moritz for the day on the train. We reached our destination and were standing on the road below the town when I heard, from the other side of a wall of ice, an extraordinary sound, the violent rattle of tin on steel. I knew at once this was the bobsleigh run, because my father, a famous Cresta rider in his day, had told me about it. I looked over as a bob came hurtling past and decided: This is exciting, This is for me.

In case there should be any confusion, I should explain that there are two runs from St Moritz down to a little village called Celerina.

22 The Prince of Nepal (left) and Johnny at St Moritz, 1948.

There's the St Moritz Tobogganing Club run (the Cresta Run, started by the English, who else!), down which you go, on a skeleton, as it is called, lying on stomach and chest, head first, with your nose about six inches up from solid ice, at speeds up to 80 m.p.h.

Then there's the St Moritz bobsleigh run, again a British invention, for big, heavy sleighs carrying either two men (a boblet) or four (the bob). The bob carries a driver, two men in the middle, and a brake at the back, crew and bob together weighing about half a ton. The bigger and heavier the four men are, the better for speed, as you scream down at up to 80 m.p.h., round terrifying hair-pin bends and down giddy gradients—in the mile and a quarter run, there is a drop of something like 2,000 feet.

We were all aware of the dangers. In my day there was a fatal accident at least once every three or four years, usually caused by the bob leaving the run at a steep bend and catapulting itself and its crew into the wide blue yonder. That's what happened to a friend of mine, who was catapulted into a tree and died outright—and he was on his honeymoon! Nonetheless I had my first run the morning after I'd been persuaded to sign up by Lawrence Pratt, ex-Cambridge Blue at the quarter mile, whom I had met there at St Moritz. And I loved it.

I became good at it too, good enough to beat Nino Bibbia, an Italian who lived in St Moritz and who won a gold on the Cresta in the 1948 Olympics, as well as several other awards.

In the next couple of years, I was to go over the top with my team mates four times. Inevitably we were all pretty well knocked about and not a few bones broken—but at least the fates decreed that none of us would be killed. The great thing is that you get such a kick out of it—and the girls think you are marvellous, which is one of the reasons for doing it.

One afternoon I was sitting in the grand foyer of the Palace, having a cup of tea. Suddenly a whole lot of enormous great men in flying jackets and boots trundled in, and I realised that they were the English bobsleigh team. Among them was Mike Holliday, wartime fighter-pilot ace and a terrific character, who was to become a very great friend and an inseparable team member on the bob runs.

Later I was to be his best man at his wedding in London to airline receptionist Pamela Phillips. We had one hell of a stag night, fell into bed at about 6 a.m.—and had to drag ourselves out just two hours later because it was a morning ceremony. We both looked as bad as we felt—pale and pissed. Still, we got to Belgravia on time and managed to behave like gentlemen.

It was only a couple of days after that first encounter in the Palace foyer that Mike and a couple of his colleagues took me down the

23 Sqn Ldr Mike Holliday and Johnny winning the Pasha Gold Cup at St Moritz in January 1949.

bobsleigh run. It was from that moment that my passion for the sport took off in earnest, and I became a member of the team.

From the start I rode number one as the driver, with numbers two and three (who push at the start with the fourth member of the team) in the middle and Mike's dependable 16 stone as the back (a solid weight helps acceleration) as brakeman.

When I came to represent England, I was doing so because I was the best. King of the Bobsleigh, they'd dubbed me. That isn't arrogance. It's honesty. When the Olympics in Norway were coming up, I'd earned the telegram from Mike which reached me at the Guards Club in Mayfair and gave me the biggest accolade I could ever have asked for: 'Satisfactory meeting Martineau'. (Hubert Martineau was chief of the British Bobsleigh Association.) 'Congratulations. You are definitely in Olympic team St Moritz. No good without you. Mike.'

All this was all a long time ago, but once you've experienced bobsleighing, you can never forget the terrific adrenalin surge, and the stomach-clenching mix of sheer terror and wild exhilaration. It's difficult to put into words, but I'll try.

The driver is sitting at the wheel, with his numbers two and three slowly easing the bob backwards and forwards on its highly polished steel runners, to prevent any ice or snow sticking to them. Then the driver turns round and says, 'OK boys, let's go!'.

Numbers two and three and the brakeman then pull the bob backwards and forwards three times and on the third time they go. When they go they run flat out, pushing with every pound of weight they have, because a split second gained at the top can make a very big difference.

Imagine you're riding number two on the bob and going down the run for the first time in your life. You sit there hanging on grimly and tightly to the handles. The faster you go, even with the modern suspension the bobsleighs have, the rougher the ride seems to get. All you can hear is the wind, and ice particles cracking off the run as the steel runners bite into it on the corners. The noise is like a lot of tin pots and pans being violently rattled together, as the machine hurls its way down the mile long run.

The first few bends are quite harmless and not terribly sharp. Then suddenly you see facing you an enormous curved ice wall, perhaps twenty feet high and thirty yards long. It appears as if you are going to go straight through it and out the other side. But no, banked up to 90 degrees, round goes the bob, and a split second later you're going the reverse way. By now you are a third of the way down the run and picking up speed every second.

The whole run then seems like an agony. A kaleidoscope of blue sky, ice and snow, and the whole time the crunch, crunch, as the runners bite into the polished ice. You go right, you go left, you do another 180 degree turn and find you are going the opposite way again. You feel your stomach and your whole body being pressed into the seat of your pants as you get a terrific gravity force on these hairpin bends. Your body is three times the weight of gravity.

At last you reach the last few hundred yards of the run, which is usually the steepest part, and you feel as if you're going down into the very bottom of hell itself. You think: 'I shall never get off this machine alive', and suddenly you realize it is the end of the run and the bob is travelling at 80 m.p.h.

The driver shouts 'Brake!'. You are going uphill on the run-out and slowing down, and the brakes, like small dragon teeth, are biting into the track. You come to a halt and you get off the bobsleigh. You feel like a hero, and as you drive back up to the top and all the girls wave at you, you think: 'This is a man's sport'. And it is, and you want to go again.

Mike was just as obsessive. A witty *Evening Standard* writer named John Waterman summed him up succinctly: 'Holliday has no other hobbies. And during the long summer days in England his favourite occupation is looking at pictures of bobsleighing—and waiting impatiently for winter.'

But as I've already indicated, we paid dearly for our enthusiasms in terms of broken bones, gashes, bruises and body-racking aches and pains. The two most dramatic incidents came within 24 hours of each other. On the first day I crashed a two-man bob and came out of it with a couple of cracked ribs and multiple bruises. All the medics could do with the ribs, of course, was to strap me up. Mike was my brakeman, and luckily he was thrown clear and uninjured.

The next day was the four-man Championships of Switzerland event, and I was doggedly determined to use it to win a place in the British bobsleigh team for the World Championships. That meant that every split second counted.

So, groaning ribs or not, Mike and I and our fellow team members, London banker Roy Seel, and William McCowan, a young Cambridge undergraduate friend, were clear that we should go for maximum speed. We were going brilliantly, screaming down at more than 80 m.p.h.—in fact, up to that point, we were breaking the track record for the season.

Then disaster hit us at almost the same spot as on the previous day, on the steep finishing stretch. I lost control, soared up the side of the track and over the ice parapet and, quite literally, took off. The bob somersaulted twice, and catapulted me through the air to thud into a snow bank. The impact didn't do my ribs much good, and inflicted a good deal of surface damage elsewhere.

My team mates were hurled out onto the ice track itself, and shot the rest of the way down and over the finishing line on their faces. Roy escaped with minor bruises, but Mike and William joined me in hospital with cuts, lacerations and a cracked wrist.

A chap from London's *Evening News* rang the hospital next day and Mike—'in a muffled, suffering voice'—spoke for all of us: 'My body is black and blue all over and my nose, which was cut to shreds, is now swollen to bursting point and hurts like blazes. My ribs and bones ache just everywhere when I breathe. Johnny Kimberley feels exactly the same and is just as miserable as I am.' By then, despite deep facial cuts, Roy Seel had left for Zurich.

But Mike still wasn't finished. Of the fated run he observed: 'We were going fast, far too fast really, and were asking for trouble. Johnny is a real dare-devil driver and doesn't care a hang'.

There's loyalty for you! Though on one thing we did agree: Neither of us could wait to get back and on to a sleigh again. That, reasonably, took a few days—but the day after being whisked off to hospital, we were back beside the run, keeping up to date with the racing.

Inevitably, once I was back behind the driving wheel, there were other crunches to come. The one that put me out of action longest was a badly broken leg, which came, as we shall see, at a most inconvenient juncture. Though before that fated time arrived, there were other diversions which still crowd pleasantly upon the memory.

It was through bobsleighing, in fact only a couple of days after my first run, organised by Lawrence Pratt, that I met Gretchen Merill, American figure skating champion of 1948. She was terribly attractive, wonderfully sexy, quite beautiful, and was in St Moritz to compete in an Olympic skating event.

I fell madly in love with her, she wanted me as much as I wanted her, and we had an all-too-brief but memorable affair—a real case of young love, she a nubile 19 and me an eager 22. One night, when she had a skating event coming up the next day, she said she needed to rest before skating. I said she'd be much more relaxed if she had a good night of love-making instead. She tried my theory. But she didn't get a gold. That year it went to a Canadian girl.

When the time came for us both to leave St Moritz, she told me she was going to Paris, before heading home across the Atlantic. I

24 Gretchen Merill, American figure skating champion at the 1948 Olympics.

returned to London, but couldn't get her out of my mind. So I flew to Paris to find her again. We stayed together at the Ritz and had a wonderful time. I tried hard to persuade her to come and live with me, but she didn't want to come to England.

So sadly we parted, and once more I was back in London, with only a sheaf of photographs to remember her by. I showed them to my mother. 'Yes, she's nice', she said. 'But I hope you weren't thinking of marrying her.' As well she might, for my non-marriage to Diana was barely 16 months old.

In those days I used to smoke Benson & Hedges cigarettes, which were sold in distinctive square, red tins. I always carried a tin in my hip pocket, and had one there when I drove to Northolt Airport—which was where one flew from to Paris in those days, by British European Airways—to rejoin Gretchen.

But it contained more than cigarettes. At that period, so soon after the war, no-one was allowed to take more than £25 in cash out of the country, and there were heavy penalties if you were caught exceeding the limit. Nonetheless I'd taken a chance, and had a couple of big value notes, folded and placed under the cigarettes. I also had about £300-worth of travellers' cheques that I'd won from an American, playing backgammon in St Moritz.

That is a game at which I've been adept since childhood, when I learned to play it with my mother. I nearly always won even then, though she probably let me. In any event, she invariably paid up—£1 a game, which was quite a lot for a little boy!

Anyway, on the plane I was duly handed the usual immigration form to fill in, declaring how much money in cash and travellers' cheques I was carrying into France. I declared amounts within the limit, but no more! I got off the aeroplane, and stepped into one of the coldest nights of the year. I was wearing a camel hair overcoat, but was still freezing cold. A French customs man called me over and said:

'You will come with me please!'

As I followed him, expecting the worst, I had visions of a night in the cells at Le Bourget rather than a comfortable bed at the Paris Ritz. He frisked me, tapped my back pocket and asked:

'Boite de cigarettes?'

'Oui.'

But he didn't ask to see it, and waved me on.

When things went smoothly and they'd accepted that you were carrying only the allowed £25, you might be asked how you would be financing your stay in France. I'd always taken the precaution of making a lot of well-heeled European friends at St Moritz who, realising my currency position, would generously insist that, when I was in Paris, I should stay as their guest at the Ritz or wherever, and would set this down in writing.

I always carried several of these invitations in my briefcase. But they wouldn't have helped at all if that customs man at Le Bourget had discovered what I was really carrying that night.

The currency difficulties were a real bind. But there were ways round them, if you knew the ropes. And the keepers of those ways were the head porters in the top hotels, like George at the London Ritz who eased my clothing coupons problems during the war. But their network wasn't just on home ground. It was—probably still is—international.

So you'd consult your chosen head porter with the passwords: 'I owe Max £50', give him £50 in fivers in an envelope on which was written 'Max Exchange', and he through his network would do the deal for you and the bill would be paid in local currency. How it worked one didn't know, and certainly didn't ask.

At one period, I was in St Moritz for about eight weeks, staying at the Kulm Hotel, and throughout my stay had signed all the bills. When the day of my departure came, I asked Tony Badrutt, owner and director of the hotel:

'Do you want me to pay the head porter at Claridge's or the Ritz?'

'But Johnny', he replied, 'you have been here for eight weeks'.

'But Tony, surely you didn't think I could get by on a British currency allowance. How did you think I was going to pay?'

It was then that Tony astonished me by suggesting that a man named Ronnie Cornwell could guarantee my bill. I already knew him, and about his disreputable character. In fact I'd met him in St Moritz, though I wasn't aware at that moment that he also was staying in the Kulm.

'Are you sure that's what you want?' I asked. 'I hope you're not making a mistake.'

But when Tony insisted, I agreed—and hoped he knew he was dealing with a character who was known as the biggest conman in Europe. I made out a cheque for £500 to Ronnie Cornwell, post-dating it so that I would be back in England when it was presented. That way, I wouldn't be committing a currency offence, and opening myself up to the possibility of a £1,000 fine or even a jail sentence.

I was back at Kimberley when the telephone rang a few weeks later. It was Tony Badrutt, calling on a terrible line from St Moritz.

'Johnny, you were right. Not only did Cornwell not pay your hotel bill. He didn't pay his own either.'

'I'm sorry', I responded, 'but that is your own bloody fault'.

I was more than a bit sour about this whole business, so I went up to London and discovered where Cornwell's office was in Bond Street. It was in a building where there were brass plaques right down the jambs on each side of the main entrance, with Cayman Islands and other dodgy tax haven addresses.

I found Cornwell's door and walked straight in to a smutty outer office, where a secretary jumped up and tried to head me off saying 'He's not in!'. She tore after me as I ignored her and headed straight for the next door, which I pushed open, revealing Ronnie sitting behind a desk with his feet up on it, his shoes playing centrepiece to a quartet of telephones, red, white, blue and green respectively.

He was smoking an enormous cigar, and beside him was an open bottle of brandy and a well-used glass—this at 2.30 in the afternoon. After a second of shock, he slapped on a conman's smile and welcomed me with a breezy 'Hallo Johnny, how nice to see you'.

I was in no mood for false niceties and snapped: 'You owe me five hundred bloody quid. What's more, if you don't pay me, I'm going to have you beaten up'.

'But I had to pay a currency fine, which is why I cashed your cheque', he claimed.

Having no money to pay the fine, he'd cashed my cheque and used my money, all £500 of it. But I made it plain that his troubles didn't mollify me one little bit.

'Look', he said, in a glib gambler's bid to get himself out of trouble, 'I've got a horse running next Saturday. It'll win and you can get a bit back on it'.

'I don't give a bugger what you do, but you bloody well pay up. If you don't, I've got some boys I know who will make you look a different shape'.

He did pay up eventually, though not with much help from that horse of his. It happened to be running at my local course at Fakenham in Norfolk, where it did win its race. But it was at 6-4 on, so neither he nor I was going to get much back out of that. Ronnie's dead now. Way back, I met his son at St Moritz, when he was 19 and I was about 24, a very shy, very unassuming lad. Some years later we met again in London—though by that time he was known by a different name: John le Carré.

We enjoyed together one of the most hilarious lunches I've ever had in my life. I told him stories about his father which he didn't know. He told me stories about Ronnie which I didn't know.

For example, he told me that at one point Ronnie had been prospective Liberal parliamentary candidate for Yarmouth. He didn't get in. He got arrested instead, for fraud, I think. On another occasion he hired a Rolls Royce and a grand house beside the racecourse for the Ascot meeting. But they had to pack up and run at 3 o'clock in the morning because the bailiffs were coming in.

John le Carré invited me to stay with him at his home, but sadly I never have, nor have I seen him again since that memorable lunch session. I know his address and phone number and one day I will take up the invitation. I'll never forget that afternoon as we kept on capping each other's stories.

I've already admitted that the years in which I repeatedly visited St Moritz and the Palace provided one of the happiest and most exciting periods of my life, a time of revelling in the dangers of bobsleighing and of becoming good at the Cresta run; of meeting hordes of fascinating people, enjoying a glittering social scene of a kind now virtually extinct, of forming friendships that have lasted a lifetime.

And not least, of meeting beautiful women who added colourful cameos to the fairly picaresque life I led for so long.

A browse through my photo albums would reveal a lot of pictures of one particularly beautiful woman who featured in one of those cameos. Alison Talan was her name, a married lady, though who her husband was I never knew. She was in St Moritz, when our paths first crossed, in the company of Otto Lucas, who was the leading women's hat maker in London at that time, and extremely rich. I'd first met him some years earlier in London, where he had a flat in South Audley Street. Close by was my mother's house, which was bombed during the war.

I was invited round for a drink, but my mother was rather worried about it. For he was, after all, a homosexual (the word 'gay' hadn't entered the lexicon then) who had a boyfriend living in his apartment—and I was a tender 17-year-old. But I went, nonetheless, and survived the experience unscathed, if that is the word.

When I encountered Alison, I was struck at once by how decorative, funny and intelligent she was, how beautifully she played the piano and—as I was soon to find—how wonderful she was in bed. I danced with her at the Palace the night I met her and, for want of a better expression, never looked back. Our affair lasted on and off for

25 Alison Talan, a girlfriend of Johnny's.

the next couple of years.

I don't know why, because we got on so well together, but the question of her becoming my next countess never arose.

We often stayed in Otto's lovely house in Sussex at the weekend. He was a very good host, and spoke with a fascinating, guttural accent. As we came downstairs in the morning he was wont to enquire, in his distinctive tones: 'Did you have a good fuck?'. I suppose, with his pretty boy in residence, I could have asked him the same thing.

A glimpse across a crowded room in St Moritz (which sounds like a cue for a song in a romantic musical comedy) was to lead a few months later in London to an astounding encounter whose every detail, nearly half a century later, remains clearly graven on my memory. The woman I had spotted so briefly was not beautiful, but she had an extraordinary, magnetic attraction.

I did not know who she was, but was soon to learn that she was the sister of the King of Iraq, who with his family earlier that year had been butchered in the revolution which overtook his country. The princess, by a kind touch of fate, had chosen that week to fly to New York, and thus escaped the massacre.

Months later I walked into Claridge's in London, and in the restaurant instantly recognised her seated at a table, lunching with a couple of people I knew. I walked over and was introduced. I looked at her and, almost before I'd realised what I was saying, I asked:

'I don't suppose you are free for dinner tonight?'

Looking levelly back at me, without the merest hesitation she replied:

'Yes, I am'.

We dined together at the best restaurant in town, went on to the 400 Club, and around midnight we were wrapped in each other's arms on the dance floor. I murmured to her: 'We're wasting time here. Let's go home'.

She came back to my flat and we had the most marvellous, stupendous night of lovemaking that I ever had in my life. The next morning she left for America and we never saw each other again. It was one of those extraordinary flashes of lightning. It had never happened before and would never happen again. She knew, and I knew, that it was going to be the only time.

It would be asking too much of the gods to expect each and every visit to St Moritz to spark encounters with such memorable women

26 Otto Lucas, milliner.

as Gretchen, Alison and the princess. But what the Palace did guarantee, when the day's winter sports were over, was sparkling entertainment, bubbling fun and the finest service, cuisine and wine that the world could offer. If you were rich enough that is—and there were plenty who were. And what fun we had.

At the Savoy's American Bar in London, barman extraordinary Harry Craddock created his inspired White Lady cocktail of two shots of gin, a shot of Cointreau, and a teaspoon of egg white and sweetened lemon juice, which was then shaken, not stirred.

It became a staple favourite at the Palace, and one White Lady (two would bring down a bull elephant) and champagne at dinner were enough to put into party mood everybody from debs to duchesses, and millionaire tycoons to super-rich Arab princelings. So it was no surprise to have a crocodile of the world's wealthy doing the cha-cha-cha over the bar, over the tables, through the lounge and back to the bar.

An added touch of entertainment, possibly after two White Ladies, might be to watch 'that dashing peer Lord Kimberley' (as the *Daily Express* gossip columnist reported) and his friend Squadron Leader Mike Holliday nonchalantly munching wine glasses at the bar!

I saw someone doing this at a cabaret one night and thought: If he can do it, so can I. And Mike, being as mad as me, decided he'd have a go too, though neither of us would try it unless we were past the

27 Otto Lucas's boyfriend Rolf.

sobriety barrier. The secret is to choose only wine glasses—anything else is too thick—and to take big, bold bites. If you do it gently, you get cut.

During one week in winter 1957 I recall among the gathering three stunningly beautiful Zurich mannequins—at least that's what they called themselves—named Rita, Inez and Katia. They may not have been among the rich when they arrived at St Moritz, but they were certainly much better off by the time they left. For they were 'booked' as partners by King Saud's brother, Prince Aziz, his cousin Prince Khalid, and their accompanying equerry, who each carried a sackful of solid gold coins, and spent them faster than the champagne flowed at their tables.

One Christmas, the place was seething with celebrities and titles and the gossip writers were in a feeding frenzy:

> At a crowded Boxing Night soirée I spotted Charles Clore, the London real estate millionaire; Stavros Niarchos, the Greek shipping millionaire who has rented a whole floor of the hotel; Mr and Mrs Loel Guinness and the Gaekwar of Baroda.
>
> Of the other names here Lord Kimberley, that dashing peer, and his friend ex-RAF Wing Commander Michael Holliday, have been having a gay time with two pretty American debs. Now they are calling Lord K. and his chum '1958's Dancing Champs of St Moritz', after a marathon cha-cha with their two friends which lasted for three and a half hours.

Another gossip columnist, having listed all these, outdid the Joneses by spotting Prince Henry Fuerstenberg, and Baroness Theresa von Thyssen, first wife of the German steel millionaire.

But the social ritual still had a ceremony to observe, that of New Year's Eve, which our punctilious chronicler related. 'At midnight the lights will go out', he or she breathlessly told the waiting world. 'They will come on again, accompanied by the squeaks of a (well washed) pink sucking pig, generously given by Charles Oppenheimer, which socialites will rush to touch for luck.' Such were we glitterati of the Palace Hotel. What useful lives we led!

Still, we had our practical daytime pursuits, playing heroes on the bobsleigh run. Though that, you will recall, repaid me with a very badly broken leg—which came just when I was deeply involved with Carmel Maguire, whom I'd met on the Isle of Wight and with whom

I become instantly involved in a whirlwind romance.

As St Moritz meant so much to me, I took her there to enjoy it with me—and it was there that I proposed to her. She accepted, and in no time we'd decided that it seemed a romantic place in which to get married, with all the sleighs and horses and snow and fairy lights.

Before the chosen day we were there at the Palace Hotel a full month, during which we shared a double room. On the day we were married the hotel pushed the beds together, which was rather sweet of them. The honeymooning days that followed did not stop me from bobsleighing, which was enough for the gods to smile ironically and influence events.

For no sooner had we taken our vows, till-death-us-do-part, than I smashed my leg, and pretty badly too. Still, there was no good reason for letting it get in the way of my activities.

Now in order to drive a bob, one needs to sit with legs slightly bent, as when driving a car. With a straight-out, plaster-wrapped leg, it was clear that bobbing was out. So I asked the doctor to set the leg bent! Quite rightly, he refused: but he still made a bungle of the job as it was. When he applied the plaster to my leg, he omitted to leave space for the limb to swell.

And swell it did, within its unyielding armour plating. The result was horrendous agony. So at two in the morning the doctor had to be dug out, and he came round to the hotel with an enormous pair of pliers to cut off the plaster. Even that he couldn't do properly, for as he sliced away, the pliers were gouging deeply into my broken leg. It was torture and I was screaming in pain.

The gods, as life teaches us, do nothing by halves. For the taste of purgatory I suffered that night could not have been a more appropriate augury of married life with Carmel.

FIVE

THE BRIGHTEST BLADE IN BURKE'S

Carmel Maguire, Australian. Father, Mickey Maguire, his country's ex-welterweight champion. He had a cauliflower ear and knew a lot about racehorses, and was well acquainted with all the Australian jockeys and trainers. In fact he taught me more about racing than anyone else in my life. When I met Carmel at her sister's home on the Isle of Wight, she was strikingly beautiful, and I was hooked at once. She was one of five daughters of the potent Mr Maguire, and all were stunners, who took London Society by storm and became known as the Lovely Maguires.

Sister Lupe married car-hire king Godfrey Davis, and when he died he left the bulk of his £500,000 fortune to her, a tidy sum in 1960. Sister Patricia married Lord Beaverbrook's younger son, Captain Peter Aitken, who died in 1947. Sister Mary did well for herself in films. What happened to the fifth Lovely Maguire I have no idea.

Attraction for me was, and still is, visual—I just can't resist a beautiful woman. But one wants to have conversation too, and to share laughter and friends and the social round, in the country and in London. To begin with, Carmel brought me all these things. After our marriage we lived in the gardener's cottage at Kimberley, because the hall was still being restored following its appallingly destructive use during the war by the Army. The cottage was tiny, but we had a lot of fun there, and for the first couple of years we lived comparatively peacefully, and got on very well together.

Carmel took to the life of a countess with ease. She used to go shooting with me, and was very popular with my friends in Norfolk, because she had a hell of a lot of charm. She also had a violent temper, was over-fond of the bottle and chain smoked, which increasingly had their inevitable effect on our married bliss. But the real troubles were still up ahead.

A regular guest at my shoots in those years was my cousin and dear friend, Ros Harris, who reminds me that she was at Kimberley when I heard that an aunt of mine had died in Hampshire. I decided I must attend the funeral, and Ros came with me. We were held up

28 Johnny and Carmel's wedding, St Moritz, 1949.

on the way and were so late when we arrived that the funeral service was over and the burial had taken place. It was pouring with rain, but Ros relishes telling the tale that I made the priest conduct the service and burial all over again—and the reverend gentleman was not pleased.

In a small village on the Suffolk coast Ros still has a little house and studio—she's a highly talented sculptor—to which she retreats from her home in London. Long gone is a country club on the edge of the village where, she says, I came for dinner with her one evening, didn't like the music they were playing—and smashed all the gramophone records. Conveniently, I recall neither this incident, nor being persuaded by Ros to apologise and pay for replacements.

On another tack, which puts me in a rather better light, Ros recalls the pleasure she had in helping to get the church in Kimberley village ready for the harvest festival. A job made easier, she says, by the entertainment I provided by playing cheerful tunes from popular musicals on the church organ. I've never studied music in my life but, like my father before me, I've struggled to play by ear, classics, songs, anything, and generally to the approval of those who listened.

A couple of friends whom Carmel invited up to Kimberley were

29 A shooting party at Kimberley. Left to right: Sir Jocelyn Beauchamp, Jack Young-
man, Wendy Cherry (child), Gene Cherry, David Cherry, Carmel (with dog), Stanhope
Joel, Gerry Bullard, Dickie Gaskell, Colin McLean.

Victor Hervey, then Lord Jermyn and later the Marquess of Bristol,
and his wife Pauline, a very luscious looking blonde. Her second
husband was Teddy Lambton, well-known Newmarket trainer in the
years immediately after the war, who took over the Kremlin Stables
from his famous father, the Hon. George Lambton.

Victor was a considerable character whom I liked very much. He
was very funny and there was always laughter about him. He had the
questionable distinction of being one of the Mayfair Playboys, as they
became known, a group of pre-war, playboy jewellery thieves in the
Raffles tradition. At length the law caught up with them, and the
scion of one of England's great landed families ended up in jug.

Entertaining, Victor unquestionably was. But he could also be
something of an embarrassment. He would get up on his feet in some
smart London restaurant and shout out: 'Fuck 'em all. Fuck 'em all'.
It was slightly off-putting! He also gave way to this odd temptation
when aboard his boat, which was permanently moored on the
Thames, downstream from Hampton Court.

It was a very smart, ex-Royal Navy launch, and extremely
comfortable with its eight cabins, each with a shower. From its deck,
he would bellow through a loud hailer his expletive order to the
world around him, often while indulging in another of his curious
habits, which was chucking the family silver into the swirling muddy

30 Lord and Lady Jermyn at Ickworth.

river. Why he did it I never knew. Probably he just liked throwing
things overboard.

As far as I know, no-one has ever sent a frogman down there.
There should be quite a little hoard waiting to be collected. More to
the point, that boat was to play a central role in the break-up of my
marriage with Carmel.

When Victor and Pauline came up to Kimberley, I suggested that
the next morning Victor might like to go for a walk around the estate
with me. I'd lend him one of my guns and we could shoot a few
pheasants. When morning came, he appeared for breakfast dressed in
a blue pin-striped suit.

'Are you ready to go', I asked in some puzzlement.

'Yes, I am', he replied firmly.

So out we went, to be greeted by my keepers. I couldn't bring
myself to look at them to see what their reaction would be to this
strange City gent. We walked acres of muddy fields of sugar beet and
stubble, and an odd group we must have looked. Victor made no
complaint, and no further mention was made of the matter.

There is no limit to the Bristol family's eccentricities, which go
back in an unbroken line for two or three centuries. Some years on
from that morning at Kimberley I attended a shoot at Victor's equally
eccentric family pile, Ickworth House, a few miles outside Bury St
Edmunds in Suffolk, a vast, cold, draughty place which is centred on

a looming dome akin to that of St Paul's Cathedral.

With Victor's permission, he on this occasion properly dressed in a shooting suit, I arrived with a lady friend, one of that long progression who have touched my life briefly through the years. We were conducted up to our room and there discovered a notice board, worded in military command tradition. 'There are 4 Land Rovers, green, red, yellow and blue, numbered 1 to 4 respectively', it declared. 'Guns 1 to 3 will travel in Land Rovers 1 and 2. Their loaders will travel in the other two vehicles.' Sir!

It was easy to see that all this would work fine—until a Land Rover got stuck. And inevitably, deep in Ickworth woods, one did. One carrying the loaders. Naturally the second loaders' vehicle stopped to help their afflicted colleagues—and stuck in its turn. By now the disarmed guns were in position, but still waiting for their loaders. The drive was started. Some 500 pheasants sailed over the line—and there wasn't anyone able to fire a shot at them. Unbelievable.

The quirky earl-bishop who designed and built the big house (he was Earl of Bristol between 1779 and 1803, and also Bishop of Derry from 1768) would probably have loved it, because discomfiting and embarrassing his guests was something that gave him considerable humorous satisfaction. On one occasion he had a particularly rich living to bestow and invited the fattest of his clergy to dinner. They feasted greedily until they groaned—whereupon he sent them off on a cross-country run to decide who should get the living. Carefully he'd chosen a route over boggy ground, which left the overweight priests floundering in the mud. Not one reached the winning post.

The bishop found it vastly entertaining. What his exhausted and humiliated guests thought is another matter. Such was the gene inheritance of the Bristol clan.

In due time, Victor and Pauline produced John, heir to the marquessate. He was to grow into a young man who, in a long blaze of publicity, followed in Victor's footsteps to prison, and brought down not only the family fortune but its name too, until the day he died. He expired, alone, in 1999, in a farmhouse on the estate. The verdict was death through chronic drug abuse on which he is said to have spent £7 million over 25 years.

Understandably, when I had married Carmel, I wanted a son and heir too. Unhappily Carmel had several miscarriages. Then she was pregnant again, and all seemed to be going well—except that she

31 Johnny and spectators at the World Bobsleigh Championships, Garmisch, 1951.

smoked and drank her way through the pregnancy. Anyway, we pipped the Jermyns to the post by about four years.

Rows were already a regular part of our life, but it was at this time that we had a particular clash. I mentioned earlier my delight at getting that telegram from Mike Holliday confirming 'You are definitely in the Olympic (Bobsleigh) team. No good without you'. Now the time had come, and I was due to leave for Alpe d'Huez in France with my team mates for the world championships. Carmel and I were in London and she flared at me, ferociously:

'If you leave me here, pregnant, I will get rid of you.'

I told her she was being thoroughly unreasonable. I tried to coax her round by pointing out that if my father had been going to play polo for his country in America, when my mother was pregnant with me, Mother would have said: 'Go, darling, and play well'. But she was determined to stop me competing for Great Britain.

She would not relent, and to keep the peace, and to protect our child she was carrying, I gave way. I did then what I was often to do to escape marital frictions. I flung out of the house and went in search of some diversion. With Mike Holliday I went to Churchill's nightclub, where I met a girl named Caryl Chance. And what a chance it was. She became a very great love in my life, a bit of a nutcase and irresponsible, but I adored her. It was the start of a terrific affair

32 Johnny (centre) with Mike Holliday.

which lasted on and off for about three years.

A few weeks later I saw off my team mates at Victoria Station, where I was photographed with them. I watched, wretched, as the train pulled out, taking with it my big chance to grab the ultimate bobsleigh crown. But at least I had Caryl to take my mind off things. She was tall, had a fascinating face, a marvellous sense of humour—and was really terrific in bed.

It was through her that I met a highly entertaining Bohemian crowd, among them Lucian Freud, who through the Fifties and Sixties was one of the foremost modern artists of his day. Goodness knows why, but I never bought any of his paintings at the time. They'd be worth a fortune now. Caryl wrote to me regularly, but it all had to be very clandestine, so her letters were addressed to the home farm on the Kimberley estate so that Carmel wouldn't see them.

Tensions at home with Carmel reached such a point that, on the orders of my doctor, I had to have an agreement with her that I must get away on holiday from time to time, otherwise I would have a nervous breakdown. It was on one of these 'away days', when tensions were at breaking point, that I shot off to the south of France with Caryl and had a wonderful break.

My son and heir, John, Lord Wodehouse, was born on 15 January 1951. He was always a weak little boy, and through his life has been sorely troubled by bad eyesight. Who is to know whether Carmel's drinking and smoking while she was carrying him were contributory factors. Still, despite our frictions, we stayed together three years. Though there was one near miss which, had Carmel known, would have provoked another titanic explosion of temper and an even quicker end to our marriage.

We were staying in a friend's borrowed flat in London. One evening I slipped out to see Caryl at a pub round the corner. When I returned to the flat I glanced in a mirror and saw to my dismay that there was lipstick all over my collar. Carmel saw it too and—thank God—she thought it was her lipstick, and apologised for letting me go out without her spotting it. If only I'd known, I was on much stronger ground than I'd realised.

By this time, though we were both officially still living at Kimberley in the cottage, I spent a lot of time away in London where I'd acquired a flat. It meant that Caryl and I could see a lot of each other, although we weren't living together. I regularly used to get in the car at about four in the morning, and drive back to Kimberley, arriving at around 7.30. After some breakfast I'd meet my shooting party and take them off for a day's shoot. At the end of the day, as often as not, I'd return to London. In retrospect, nobody seemed to find my curious timetable in the least odd.

One evening I was driving up from London with one of my greatest friends, Derek Le Poer Trenche. He was a delightful fellow whom I'd first met at Eton. He was my age and we became good friends at once. Later he regularly came up to Kimberley to shoot, and I hunted with him in Ireland on one of his horses, including a splendid animal named Sir Humphrey, which I bought from him and brought home.

He had a large country house in Galway, called Woodlawn, which was one of the coldest houses I've ever been in, with huge rooms, no central heating, tiny Victorian fireplaces but not many fires—as he had no servants, there was no one to tend them.

He rode with the famous hunt, the Galway Blazers, whose master was Philip Profumo, brother of Jack (John) Profumo, the politician who was disgraced during the Macmillan era. Philip had been a Life Guards officer, which was where he met Derek, who was in the same regiment.

Philip, I recall, had a funny little hunt terrier whose party piece was to get on to the dining table during dinner at Woodlawn, and walk from one end of the table to the other without knocking over so much as a wine glass!

On the night Derek and I were motoring up to Norfolk, we stopped off at the Cromwell Arms at Stevenage, which was a good place for dinner in those days. During dinner, Derek drank quite a lot, which was unusual for him. Towards the end of the meal I said to him:

'Derek, I'm going to have another couple of days shooting next week. Would you like to come?'

'I can't', he replied. 'I'm going down to the Punt' (which is what we all called Victor Jermyn's boat on the Thames).

By now he was rather in his cups, and when I asked him why he was going to the boat he blurted out:

'Because Carmel's going to be there. We've been having an affair.'

When I'd absorbed what he said, I hissed at him: 'You little shit'. His response was to plead that I wouldn't cite him for divorce.

Derek wasn't the kind of man I would have suspected of duplicity, yet here he was, one of my best friends, admitting to sleeping with my wife. What did shock me, even with my not exactly chaste morals, was that I knew Derek was at the same time having an affair with Victor's wife, Pauline. As for Carmel, though I didn't realise it at the time, I accepted in retrospect that if it hadn't been Derek she was carrying on with, it would have been somebody else.

It was, one must also confess, a blow to my ego. Though my bruised male pride was practical enough to recognise that this turn of events would make my life a little easier in pursuing my affair with Caryl.

Still, I hadn't been very observant. The summer before, I had sent Carmel and Derek off to the races at Newmarket on several occasions, and a mutual friend had remarked, laughing, that if the two of them were seen together many more times, people would begin to think they were having an affair. Six months later, I found it to be true. I roared with laughter at the time!

I never faced Carmel with her infidelity with Derek. It just simmered away in the background, as she continued to live in the gardener's cottage and enjoyed playing the role of Lady of the Manor. Whether Derek had told her I knew what was going on I don't know, but our encounters became increasingly acid, until the day the final breaking point came.

I was welcoming a shooting party in front of the hall, when

Carmel appeared, leading Derek's labrador, which he'd left with her at the cottage. In front of all my guests she flared: 'You don't seem to like Derek any more, so you can have his bloody dog instead'. With that she pulled off the dog's leash and, with everyone looking on, lashed me across the face with it. After that I made it clear: This is the end. Just go!

It wasn't long before she did clear out. It seems she already had another man waiting in the wings, Jeremy Lowndes, a rich City broker, whom she married after our divorce. Hardly surprisingly, with Carmel on the opposite side, the divorce was not plain sailing, especially when it came to the issue of access to my son. Carmel went out of her way to discredit me, and to convince the judge that I was unreliable, dishonest and a liar—but the ploy failed because her counsel evidently didn't do his homework. I was in the witness box under cross-examination.

'Now, Lord Kimberley. I understand that you live at Kimberley Hall. How many bedrooms do you have?'

'I haven't the faintest idea.'

'I understand that you have twelve staff.'

'No, I have three.'

'I understand that on a day's shooting, you have 12 or more servants.'

'They, Sir, are beaters, not cooks and servants.'

The whole courtroom erupted into laughter. Carmel laughed. Even the judge laughed. Clearly the nearest that learned counsel ever got to the countryside was Lincoln's Inn Fields.

Anyway, the outcome was that Carmel had custody of John, but he was able to spend the holidays with me at Kimberley. Though later, as we shall see, even that provided Carmel with grounds for complaint. When she was safely married off to Jeremy Lowndes, he rang me from London and accused me of 'bothering' her, though where and when I never tried to find out. I just told him forcefully that she was his wife now and his problem, and that he should sod off and not bother me again.

They'd obviously had a good lunch at the Mirabelle or somewhere similar, with a lot of brandy—for there was always a lot of brandy being poured when Carmel was around—and she'd probably said: 'Go and have a go at that bastard Kimberley'.

She and Jeremy settled into a villa in Spain. One night, years onward, he pushed her down the stairs and killed her, for which he did nine years for murder in Cadiz jail. But before that, Jeremy had a shot at killing himself. He put a gun against his head, pulled the trigger and sent a bullet through his skull—but it went straight through, came out the other side and he lived to tell the tale.

On the night of the fatal shove down the stairs, my son John and his wife were staying in the villa. In the early hours of the morning, Jeremy came into their room and said to John: 'I think I've killed your mother'.

So here I was, in my twenties, twice married and eligible again, though I was still seeing Caryl in London. Yet I hankered for marriage. I think I must have liked the feeling of security it gave me. So when Cynthia Abdy Westendarp came into my life, it wasn't long before the marriage cogs started to turn all over again.

We met at a Newmarket race meeting and I chatted her up. I discovered that she was a doctor's daughter from Saxmundham in Suffolk, and lived outside Ipswich with her husband Charles Westendarp—a farmer who was also a racing man and kept a stallion at stud—and their son and four daughters. She was nine years older than me, but still a very attractive woman. I was staying in Newmarket with friends who had a house in the town, and coincidentally, Cynthia was staying in a cottage at the bottom of their garden. After dinner I walked down and found her there, and there was an immediate rapport.

I invited her down to London for a couple of nights, having borrowed a flat from a friend. She turned up on the day and we had a lovely evening out on the town, and a lovely night in bed together afterwards. She then returned to her husband.

The next thing I heard was that she was ill, having contracted polio. It must have been about 12 or 13 August, because when the news reached me I was shooting grouse in Yorkshire. She had been taken to the isolation hospital at Ipswich, where her husband refused to go and see her for fear of contracting the disease. I had slept with her only just before polio was confirmed.

The friend whose flat I had borrowed panicked more than slightly, had the whole place fumigated, and accused me of being thoroughly callous in taking someone there who had a contagious disease. He just wouldn't grasp that at the time I didn't know that.

When she was released from hospital, I suggested that she should come and stay at Kimberley while she was convalescing, which she did—and never left. She and Charles Westendarp were divorced, and in the autumn of 1953 we married quietly at the register office in Norwich and Cynthia became my third countess.

We left at once for London, and spent our honeymoon night in a ghastly hotel in Curzon Street called the Washington, after which we were glad to return to Norfolk and the gardener's cottage, for the hall restoration still wasn't finished.

Cynthia was a country girl who loved horses and the countryside and was a very good rider and golfer, so she took to the Kimberley life with ease. She was up every morning early and out riding. I had started racing again and kept several horses there. We rode out together on the estate and hunted together with the West Norfolk Foxhounds. Much closer to us were the Stag Hounds, based in south Norfolk, and we greatly enjoyed riding with them.

It's hardly believable, but a couple of tame stags were kept for the hunt. They were put into a trailer, taken to the meet and then one of them was released. Off he'd go, with hounds and riders in pursuit, all having a smashing time. At a certain point, which the stag knew from experience, he'd come to a halt, and the hounds would gather happily around him—they were old friends. The stag, well exercised, would then trot back into the waiting trailer and be taken home for a good feed. No cruelty. The stags knew the country where they were running. And a good time was had by all.

To begin with, Cynthia and I enjoyed a wonderful and varied social life together. Three months before we were married I took her along with two friends when I managed to get four 'outside' tickets for the Queen's Coronation at Westminster Abbey on 2 June 1953. The day didn't start very well: one of my stupid friends opened the back door of the car as we stopped in Sloane Square, and a bus knocked it off.

After that it could only get better. As everyone who recalls that day will remember, it poured with rain, and we sat outside the abbey under a leaky awning, though we did have an excellent view. When a convenient interval in the procession came, we all went into the House of Lords and had a drink with the Marquess of Bristol, who was holding a cocktail party.

It must have been about a couple of years after that that I heard you could catch sharks off Cornwall, so Cynthia and I went down there for a few days and she, being the outdoor girl that she was, thoroughly enjoyed it. My agent in Falmouth found us a shark fishing boat that we could rent, and off we went and hauled in five small

33 John Stebbings, Pat Bagnall, Cynthia and Johnny at Falmouth.

blue sharks that day—very beautiful, but still likely to bite when you get them on to the boat. Mind you, a different league from those socking great 16 ft Great White Sharks which appeared off the Cornish coast in September 1999.

Back home at Kimberley we entertained a great deal, but it was only later that I realised what a burden I expected Cynthia to carry. She had very little help, but I suppose I took for granted our dinner parties and shooting parties and that we should stay up half the night entertaining our guests. In retrospect, she must have been absolutely exhausted.

All in all, it should have been the perfect marriage with Cynthia—if I hadn't known Caryl, which I suppose is what, in part, buggered it up. By that time, also, I was already indulging myself in the playboy life in London which was to earn me the *Daily Express* soubriquet of 'The Brightest Blade in Burke's'. You might well ask how I handled Caryl, Cynthia, a playboy lifestyle and the management of a great estate, all at the same time. The answer is: With difficulty! It was bloody hard work.

What motivated me was very simple—the whole drive was testosterone. Sex, if you must. I just couldn't think of anything else.

After all, it's the strongest instinct we have. The awful thing, as I look back, is that if Cynthia had let me off the hook occasionally, things might have been different. If I could have gone off to London, spent an evening with the boys and the night with a hostess, I would have been happy as a sandboy.

She knew what I was about when I set off for the capital. I can hear her now: 'All you want to do is to go and find some tart'. She was right.

But in my mind I wasn't being unfaithful if I just had a fuck. If she'd only given me that freedom, I'm certain I would have returned home and lived out her life with her. But she was so possessive. Too possessive. For someone like me it was like being in prison.

I remember she frightened me very much one night. I think we must have had a row and I took the car and went off to a pub in nearby Wymondham. From there I rang her but couldn't get her to answer the telephone. I drove back and found her standing by the front door of Kimberley (she insisted on moving in even before the restorations were finished) with my 20 bore under her arm. I wasn't sure whether she was going to shoot me or herself. Either way, it was very frightening. She let me take the gun away from her and was very emotional and upset.

We had been married about five years then, and I still loved her. She bore me two sons, Edward, who was born on 29 May 1954, and Henry, on 26 April 1956. It was at this juncture that Carmel reappeared briefly on the scene, endeavouring to find a way round the court ruling that my eldest boy John should spend part of his holidays at Kimberley. Carmel's view was that if he came, Cynthia would drown him in the lake so that her own son would become Lord Kimberley!

It is a sad fact that having our two sons did not bring Cynthia and me closer. Nor did the fact that, for reasons which were not to become clear until some 15 years later, she developed a distressing bad breath problem, which inevitably discouraged intimacy.

When Edward was about three, things began to come apart. We had a very good nanny to look after the boys, and that was all the excuse I needed to go off and get immersed even deeper in the London playboy whirl. So I began to neglect them.

There were terrible tensions between Cynthia and me. After a row I would just pack an overnight bag, go out to the stables to get the car, leave them all at Kimberley, and bugger off to London to enjoy

34 Johnny and Cynthia in the late 1950s.

myself. I didn't analyse my actions at the time. If I had done so, I knew I would not have liked the analysis. It is only recently that I have begun to look at myself in the mirror and to see the truth—that really I am not a very nice person.

My feelings towards Cynthia entirely changed. I knew that we had to part company. But there she was, firmly settled in at the hall. How could I be rid of her? The only way was to sell Kimberley from over her head. As far as my sons were concerned I made excuses to myself—that when they grew up, they would never be able to afford to live there anyway, or so my reasoning went.

Anyway, by now, I was so deep into the playboy scene that I was already living way beyond my immediate means and needed ready money.

For two or three months I anguished over what to do, and in desperation talked through the options with my trustees and solicitors. Finally, at my lawyer's one evening, I broke down.

'All right', I told him. 'Go ahead and sell.'

I remember him saying: 'You can't go on living like this, Johnny. You are going to run out of money completely'.

'OK, then flog it.'

At that moment, to finance my lifestyle, I was ready to cut away from a thousand years of family history, and from an estate which had been in Wodehouse hands for almost as long. I am not very proud of it. In fact I am ashamed of it. Yet I have to tell myself that if I hadn't done what I did then in the 1950s, I wouldn't be here at the turn of the 21st century in the house I love in Wiltshire, and would not be married to my adored Janey, and everything else that follows.

I admit that I felt guilty at having been the one in the Wodehouse line who cut the string. It was an agonising time. I knew every square inch of those 5,000 acres at Kimberley. The estate meant everything to me. When the press got on to it, I had a ready and self-comforting explanation: 'These big houses and estates don't have a future in the new England'.

There was another, much smaller and largely urban family estate in Falmouth, which centred on a big house overlooking the docks, Arwenach Manor, which even then in the 1950s had been turned into flats. I still have this property, which provides me with a modest income through ground rents and leaseholds. It came to us by marriage in the eighteenth century, when a Wodehouse married a lady of the Killigrew family, who owned the whole of Falmouth at that time. When my father died it passed to my mother, and she in turn made it over to me. She always said that she wished it had been the other way round, for the one place she thought I would never sell would be Kimberley. If something had to go, she believed it should have been Falmouth, which was 500 miles away at the other end of England, and meant nothing to me.

But Kimberley—house, contents, land and ancient associations (I even sold off several lordships of the manor)—all went. There was no turning back. Recently I came across a press cutting from December 1959, a good year after the estate sale, recording the auction at Sotheby's of 'an attractive suite of 12 pieces of Louis XV giltwood furniture, the property of the Earl of Kimberley. It consists of ten fauteuils and two small canapés. All the pieces are upholstered in needlework'. It went for just £3,100!

I can't remember how the final crunch came with Cynthia, just as I can't remember the final curtain in my first two marriages. I can't explain this amnesia, but it is genuine. I suppose it is a kind of psychological defence. Then came the stony road to yet another divorce.

Nearly 40 years on, I still find myself asking: Why did this marriage fail? Maybe because Cynthia was nine years older than me. Maybe because I still had Caryl nagging away at me in the background. Maybe because there is always excitement in an affair, in something that is 'illegal'.

My trustees found Cynthia a nice house near Bury St Edmunds, a large Georgian former rectory, which she furnished by stripping Kimberley of most of my furniture. But she didn't stay long at Bury. She had always had the idea that Ireland was a marvellous place in which she felt at home—she felt, she explained, some leprechaun in her blood. So off she went, found herself a house on the River Blackwater, and exported my furniture to it.

But that wasn't the end of our association. A decade or so later I received a telephone call from one of Cynthia's children. She was dying, desperately ill in hospital with cancer of the bowel. I flew over at once to Cork and went first to her house, where her children of her first marriage and our sons Edward and Henry were all staying. From there I went on to the hospital and as I walked into her room, her eyes lit up when she saw me.

She was like a little child, so thin and fragile, as if she'd been in

Belsen. 'You are going to be all right', I told her, and I believed it.

I telephoned London, on a lousy line, and got through to an old friend, Dr Tony Greenburgh, knowing I could rely on him to make the right arrangements. We got Cynthia on to an Aer Lingus flight to London that same day, and an ambulance was waiting for her as the plane touched down. From there we took her directly to a valued acquaintance, Prof. Sir Arthur Ellis, of Westminster Hospital, at that time one of the leading experts on cancer. He saw her that very night, and began to bring about an almost miraculous improvement in her. When she left Ireland she weighed five stone. Almost nine months later she left hospital, her weight back to nine or ten stone, and in no time she was playing golf again, and lived on for another 25 years.

During the time that she had been so desperately ill in Cork, I organised a rota of all of her children and myself to see that she was never left alone in her room for one minute. I stayed with her every moment I was there, and accompanied her on the plane and to Westminster Hospital, where I visited her two or three times a week without fail.

We all of us got on wonderfully well together—the children liked me, and thought I was a little god! I didn't think it was odd at the time, though now, as I consider it, perhaps I had not done much to merit such an image. But out of it all came warm friendship between all our offspring; Cynthia and I became very good friends; and the children moved happily between the two of us.

But that was in the future. With my divorce from Cynthia in 1960, I was looking back, at the youthful age of 30, at three broken marriages. Then as now, I always wanted something permanent, because I am essentially a romantic. There have to be honey and flowers and lilies and sunshine and blue skies. But I still couldn't make marriages work. All I was good at was the hedonistic, free-spending, gambling, drinking and amorous life of a playboy earl, with pockets full of money, all ready and willing to live up to the challenge, as the *Daily Express* put it, of being the Brightest Blade in Burke's.

SIX

COUNTRY LIFE

When I consider how much Kimberley meant to me, how the place flowed in my very bloodstream, the enormity of what I did in 1958 in selling up and breaking the ties of a thousand-year inheritance, shakes me even now. From early boyhood, I had learned to know and love every inch of the place: the fields and woods, the rides and shoots, the estate's abundance of feather, fur and flora. A 5,000-acre kingdom—though even then it was only half the size of what it had been a century and a quarter before.

Even that enormous house, with all its inconveniences, was a part of me. Though when I returned to it after the war, there was one presence missing, the woman who had been there, always, during my boyhood and adolescence, my old nanny, Gertrude Neat. In the late 1930s, when I no longer needed a nanny, she stayed on as housekeeper, in all but name, which was the way with most families like mine. She loved to be out in the fresh air and, carrying my cartridge bag, would often accompany me when I took my dog and went shooting on the estate for jackdaws and moorhens. She always wore a longish skirt, old-fashioned by then, as she had always done, but would stride out carrying her walking stick, which she used to tap hollow trees to make jackdaws fly out so that I could try to shoot them.

She also loved to sit on a chair beside me under an old apple tree in the orchard, when I took along my Diana airgun, which I remember cost 10s. 6d. She'd sit there for anything up to two hours, very still, otherwise the tits would not settle on the apples. When they did, I shot at them. Nanny wasn't, I have to confess, the best of shooting companions, because she always wore a white blouse, which wasn't very good for camouflage, and put up the birds.

She left us when the hall was commandeered by the military, but once a week, without fail, she wrote to me through the war years. I think she retired, and went back to live in her mother's little house near Warminster. After the war we were still in touch, and she came to my first wedding. I don't think she ever returned to Kimberley. As a child I always remembered her birthday, though I haven't a clue of the date now. We lost contact in the end, so I never knew when she died and wasn't able to attend her funeral. When I did hear of her death, it really was for me the end of an era.

It was for me also, in a very positive and wholly sincere way, also the beginning of a new era. Though if, as they say, the road to hell is paved with good intentions, then I could have paved highways across the county. No sooner was I back from the Continent than I was putting myself forward as Independent candidate for the Wymondham division of the county council and distributing manifestos which, if they make one wince now, were genuinely felt at the time. For the April 1946 election I set out my intentions with a flourish:

> I am a young man without any pre-war prejudices and I have an entirely free mind with which to help build a better post-war England; and a tradition that persuades me to devote a large part of my time and ability to public service. It is up to us, that is, you and I, to grow the best food; to build the best houses, the best schools, the best roads, and many other things; and I promise you I will do my utmost to help in all these things.

I won the seat, and stuck it out for one three-year session, after which I didn't seek re-election. I was bored and frustrated by endless talk with no vision and no real action. Nearly 55 years on, much of what we aimed for then is still waiting to happen.

In my private life, the three countesses I brought to Kimberley did not, as I've revealed, bring me unqualified happiness. But during the thirteen years after the war in which it was still in my hands, up to that fateful decision in 1958, the estate itself, whenever I turned back to it for comfort, never failed to give me joy.

Just as my father had done, I left most of the daily running of its agricultural affairs to my steward. Not long after my return from the war, a point came when I had a yearning to farm at least a part of it myself, to be a real, hands-on farmer. Also back from the war, and the rigours of being a prisoner of the Japanese, was an old friend named David Cherry, a knowledgeable farmer who had married into the wealthy Norfolk brewing family, the Bullards—his formidable Bullard mother-in-law was still riding side-saddle and following hounds at the age of 80.

I invited him to come in with me to form a partnership, in which I could provide the land, and he would bring in the expertise which I lacked. We formed a company which we called Kimberley Farms, and it all worked very effectively. After a while, though still maintaining the partnership, I had a yen to branch off on my own and do something a little different. Following something of a tussle with its sitting tenant, I got the home farm back and, after adding a few bits of land to it, soon had 400 acres in my own hands. Then I made my first move. One morning I told my steward:

'I want to keep pigs.'

'What sort, m'Lord?'

'Nice pigs', I replied.

Not in the least fazed, as they say in Norfolk, by this not exactly professional response, he suggested:

'What about Large Blacks, m'Lord?'

'I've never seen one.'

'Well, there's a smashing herd owned by Sir John Mann down at Thelveton.'

Thelveton was a village not too far away in the south of the county, so I phoned Sir John, fixed an appointment, and steward and I sallied down to see him. There was no hesitation—I bought four in-pig gilts (young pregnant sows), sent them home, then set about building a piggery, though thinking about it, perhaps I should have built it first! In the end I had 50 breeding sows and half a dozen boars.

I started showing them, and ended up with a handsome white Austin van with a Large Black painted on each side, bordered in big, bold letters with 'Kimberley Herd of Large Black Pigs'. Wherever we went to a show (and we followed them throughout both county and region, and came away with masses of awards) the van was parked strategically to show itself off to best effect, thus giving us some good free advertising.

The Royal Show, now stationed permanently at Stoneleigh, used to move to a different venue every year. During the last year in which I farmed, the show was in Norwich, and I got Champion Large Black Sow and Reserve Champion Large Black Boar, both of which I had bred. It was quite a triumph. However, when the estate went under the hammer, I had a farm sale and disposed of pigs, cattle, ploughs, everything.

As my steward had promised me, they really were nice pigs, those

35 A beautiful black lady, Kimberley Sabrina, winner of the 1st prize at the Royal Norwich Agricultural Show, 1958.

Blacks. They have lovely temperaments, and their ears grow over their eyes so they can't see where they're going, which makes it easier to contain them. They are terribly clean animals too. That is, if you let them be clean, they are clean. If you let them live in shit, then they will. So will humans! Ever since that time I've kept an affection for them. There are bronzes and sculptures of pigs in the garden here at Hailstone House in Wiltshire; and images of pigs dotted around the house. Now we humans are getting all our spare parts for our bodies from them. I love them!

During those same years, I had a passion for horses and kept several at Kimberley. Having learned to ride as a child, and continued to do so through the years, I was a pretty good horseman, and showing great promise at polo, though it was in point-to-points and steeple chasing that I made my biggest mark. Hunter trials and hunting—I followed hounds with four Norfolk hunts, the Blazers in Ireland and the Quorn in Leicestershire—were a terrific enthusiasm too.

On one hunting visit to Ireland, riding as usual a mount borrowed from Derek Le Poer Trenche (my best friend until he had an affair with my second countess), I was 'introduced' to a super little horse named Sir Humphrey. I tried him, loved him, bought him and brought him home. He was an absolute guaranteed jumper, providing you didn't get catapulted out of the saddle and fall. You didn't have to do anything: you just left it to him.

When I sold Kimberley, the house was bought by Ronald Buxton, who brought his new bride Phyllida there—and they're still there today. Ronald bought Sir Humphrey too and though he couldn't ride—he was like a sack of potatoes in the saddle—actually won a race on him. Ronald's real passion is for music—taking advantage of the spaciousness of Kimberley, he has in the house an organ, two grand pianos and a concert harpsichord.

Soon after I brought Sir Humphrey back from Ireland, I entered him in a race over the sticks at the country racecourse of Cottenham. Tiny as he was, I knew he wouldn't fall—but I soon realised that the only way I was going to win that race was in the hope that everyone else would do just that and come a cropper. We went absolutely flat out at the first fence. But better not let him get too far ahead, I thought. Needn't have bothered, because most of the field really did fall.

Finally we were approaching the last fence and there was only one horse in front of me. 'Get out of my bloody way', I yelled. The jockey looked round, which is fatal. At the last fence, he sailed out of the saddle and his horse collected itself and galloped on without him. So I won, the only horse left in the race!

On another occasion I wasn't quite so lucky. I was riding a horse called Near Dawn in the Novice Hurdle Race at Hurst Park, near Hampton Court. We fell, I came down heavily, and was carted off in an ambulance. As it happened, all I'd done, though it was pretty painful, was to break a bone in one foot.

It was several months later, riding my splendid Dick the Gee, that I had the worst fall of my riding career, though I didn't realise it right at the time it happened. After the incident, I got myself home, feeling rough, and took to my bed with a bottle of brandy. That night, at about 10.30, I felt rather better. I knew there was a hunt dance on that evening—I think it was at Lord Townshend's place, Raynham Hall. So I decided to get up, and go. My wife—it was Cynthia, my number three—tried to dissuade me. But I got up nonetheless, dressed in pink coat and white tie, and we set off. I had a couple of drinks and felt no pain at all.

Next morning when we got home I don't know how I got up the

stairs. I could barely move and was in terrific pain. It was no good, we had to call an ambulance to get me to Norwich. I saw Tommy Britten, a world-renowned orthopaedic surgeon and acknowledged as one of the best in Europe. I knew him already—when I smashed a leg very badly at St Moritz, the local quack made a real cock-up of setting it, and when I came home Tommy had to break it again and re-set it.

As soon as I'd been stretchered into the hospital he X-rayed me. My back was broken! He then hung me up by my chin and wrapped plaster round me from my upper chest to the base of my spine. So there I was in this carapace for eight months. God, I itched horribly, and kept a long knitting needle at hand to scratch. But I could still fuck—lying on my back, that is—though admittedly not with my usual vigour. After the plaster came off, I had to support my back by wearing a corset (borrowed from my trainer's wife), plus stockings and suspenders to stop the bloody thing riding up! I often wondered what would happen if I had a motor accident and was carted off to the Norfolk & Norwich Hospital, where they would discover this drag outfit beneath my clothes. Thank God, it never happened. But it could have.

Dick the Gee, mentioned a moment ago, was a lovely animal and I won several races on him. He was originally trained at Newmarket by George Archibald, an ex-jump jockey who in the 1950s owned and trained from Saville House stables, one of Newmarket's attractively traditional old yards, which still survives, unspoiled.

On Dick the Gee I won the Cottenham Members Race, and went on to win it twice more, though not on the same horse. Mine was the only name on this enormous great cup, as winner three years running, which used to be on the dining table at Kimberley. I always hoped they would at least give me a replica of it, but to my disappointment, they never did.

My ambition was to become an amateur steeplechase jockey and ride at Cheltenham and Liverpool, and to win the Foxhunters on both tracks. I had found just the horse capable of pulling off the double. He was called Elldritch, whom I bought as a yearling for just £80. He looked terribly gawky when I acquired him, so I turned him out at Kimberley for a couple of years. The result was that he grew into a tall, beautiful horse, a really magnificent animal, who jumped superbly and had a lovely temperament.

A 1953 clipping of a photograph from one of the sporting papers,

36 Johnny winning the 2½-mile steeplechase at Fakenham on Dick the Gee in 1958.

boldly captioned 'That Popular Peer of the Turf', shows me up on Elldritch and moving in fine style. Flatteringly the accompanying report predicts: 'Lord Kimberley is owner, trainer and a jockey whose horsemanship foretells successes to come'. It was tempting the gods. The week before Cheltenham, Elldritch went lame, so unfortunately he never ran there and I never rode there, though I'm totally confident he could have taken the Foxhunters.

It remains one of the regrets of my life that I never achieved either Cheltenham or Liverpool, which I would love to have done. But my greatest regret, in the sporting sphere, is not to have ridden in the Grand National. Now that would have been an experience. But unfortunately, I never owned a horse that was good enough for it.

I rode in the Grand Military Gold Cup at Sandown, though I didn't like the course much—the first fence was downhill, which was pretty nerve-racking. My very last race, before I gave up this level of riding, was at Fakenham in Norfolk. It was a very simple country course then. Now it's smartened up and very professional, and televised too, though they tell me it still keeps its friendly character and, then as now, everybody runs into their horsy and hunting friends.

From that circle there comes to me through half a century the image of a fondly remembered, sweet old boy named Col. Geoff Shaw, who was master of the North Norfolk Harriers. He was a great countryman with terrific knowledge of wildlife and every nuance of the countryside. It was he who told me the fascinating fact that a hare could produce up to eight leverets in a litter, and when she gave birth she would drop two of them in one spot, move on and drop two more, and so on. This way they had more chance of survival.

The colonel's only problem was that he was permanently pissed, though in an amiable, gentlemanly way which endeared him to everyone. The Harriers held their hunt ball in the old Lido Ballroom in Norwich, which made a lot of sense, as private houses (as misguided owners knew from dire experience) were generally ruined if they took on the event.

As master, Col. Geoff's table was elevated by about eight steps above the dance floor. On one memorable occasion he was halfway down the stairs and, as usual, benignly inebriated, when he slipped and tottered. On a banister rail there was an enormous vase of flowers. In an effort to save himself he clutched at the blooms—and master, vase, flowers and all pitched forward and came down in one almighty crash on to the ballroom floor. The occasion passed into local legend.

In those years after the war, county social life was very colourful, a round of hunts and hunter trials, local race meetings, coursing, balls, country house dinners and, very central to the scheme of things, shooting parties, which I hosted regularly at Kimberley and naturally was invited back to my friends' estates. Whatever the occasion, the wine and spirits flowed freely, for there was no breathalyser then, thank God, and one could go out, have a good time and drive 40 miles home without any problems.

Happily there is, as far as I know, no offence of being inebriated in charge of a horse. Not that I confess to the charge. My musing is prompted by an apocryphal tale, or rather a piece of local legend, which has recently come to my ears from Norfolk.

The story has it that I had a ride hacked through Kimberley's woodland, with good turf taking the place of standing timber. Legend says that I then had built for me a chariot of the Boadicea type—but without the sword blades on the wheels.

Late of a night, when I had freely imbibed (and the moon presumably was at its fullest), I am said to have hitched one of my horses to the chariot, stripped stark naked, mounted said chariot—and galloped flat out down the darkened ride.

It's such a good story, it seems a pity to have to deny it. But I must. I have a vague recollection of having heard a variation of it, but alas I cannot claim it as mine.

So back to facts! Among my many roles in the local community was the presidency of the Kimberley & Wymondham (pronounced Wind'm) Coursing Club, which usually met on my estate. I was wryly amused, on coming across a 1957 press cutting recording the club's annual dinner, to observe how the wheel turns and nothing really changes. One of the local papers reported my broadside against a small minority who were doing their level best to stop all forms 'of what they call cruel sports', and my rallying call to all present to support the work of the British Field Sports Society in their struggle against 'this nasty enemy in our midst'. Tell that to Mr Blair and New Labour's holy war against fox hunting. *Plus ça change*, indeed.

Apart from the coursing club, I presided over a bird-watching club, clay pigeon shoots, and two motoring organisations, the Snetterton Motor Racing Club (based at the nationally regarded Snetterton race track) and the Sporting Car Club of Norfolk. In addition I had close associations with everything from gymkhanas to local agricultural shows—and all of them were alive, active and well supported, giving to the living countryside a heartbeat which these days is on a life-support machine!

The Snetterton club provided some enjoyable events, guaranteed to get the adrenalin running. I had a Mark VII 3½-litre Jag, from which I had the silencers removed so that the gases went straight through from the block to the end of the exhausts. The car went like a rocket, though I never won a race with it. But I had a lot of fun. It also came in useful from time to time to join in jolly events with the Sporting Car Club, like Ten Test rallies which went on right through the night—though not always, as the club's witty little magazine underlined, with the friendly support of local residents:

> The 1953 Ten Test had to be cancelled, but 1954 and '55 Ten Tests gave us the nocturnal trials of map reading, and fighting to keep awake in the early hours. Meanwhile indignant would-be sleepers were galloping up and down the road in their pyjamas, cursing the very name of night rallies, and threatening to sue the people with the extra loud exhaust notes.

I wonder whom they possibly could have meant?

The magazine excelled itself on another occasion with the drollest of droll observations on the behaviour of short tempered competitors:

> With the commencement of the rally season, attention of all competitors is drawn to the warning in a recent edition of this magazine regarding SWEARING at gently nurtured Marshals and the penalties attached thereto ...

Again one asks oneself, to whom could he possibly have been referring? Whomever! How could anyone have been bored by country life? I certainly wasn't. There was always something new on the horizon. And yet, and yet, London and its attractions was invariably nagging just under the skin!

At Kimberley Hall, responding to the vibrant local social life of which, as a titled landowner, I was inevitably a principal cog in our locality, I had a modern kitchen installed next to the dining room, a useful improvement on the old one which was a 150-yard trek away at the opposite end of the main wing, below stairs too, and narrow, very steep stairs at that. Legend has it, though I can't confirm its authenticity, that on one occasion a serving lad got half way up the steps when the vast tureen of soup he was carrying overbalanced him, and he tumbled backwards in a shower of hot potage and shattered china.

I never employed a butler, but had a couple of girls from St

37 Johnny and Henry, his son by Cynthia, at Battersea Funfair.

Helena who looked after the house and did most of the cooking. During Cynthia's time, she often did the cooking for our frequent entertaining, and very good at it she was too. Following all the changes brought about by the war, it wasn't unusual by then for a countess to be found cooking in her own kitchen. The household staff was completed by an odd-job man who did the firewood and the like—with so many fireplaces in the house, some of them big enough to take half a tree, it was virtually a full-time job looking after them.

All the mutual entertaining came to a halt in March, with the end of the hunting season, and the migration of the county set down to Cheltenham, and on to Ascot in June. But I remember one year there was still a little hunting diversion to come—potting pigeons from the roof of Norwich cathedral, and in the bishop's garden next door. The pigeons were becoming so numerous they were a bloody nuisance, so I joined m'lord bishop, no less, and the chief constable's brother, Clare van Neck, in culling the buggers. It did cause some problems with the locals, who called the RSPCA! Clearly they had no idea who was leading the extermination brigade.

But even during these years of country pursuits and the very real enjoyment which Kimberley gave me, I was frequently in London in quest of all the city pleasures it could provide. Once my estate was gone, and my marriage to Cynthia had collapsed, the call back to all those pleasures was too strong to ignore. My first-born son John was with his mother, Carmel, as were my younger sons, Edward and Henry, with their mother Cynthia, so there was nothing to hold me back. I wasn't a very good father because I never had the opportunity to be one, and because I never had a wife who stayed with me. If I had been half as good as my own father, I would have been a marvellous parent.

John was educated at Summerfield preparatory school at St Leonards in Sussex; and then, following my footsteps, at Eton. He didn't go into the Army because of eyesight problems—he was a premature baby and has pebbledash vision. He studied very hard, became a biochemist and is a skilled computer operator. He is married and has two children in their twenties. I have a good relationship with him; we have lunch together fairly often, and frequently talk on the telephone.

I think I was a very good stepfather to Cynthia's family, who all adored me. Edward and Henry are in their forties now—Edward is in the motor business and Henry, who is based in Liverpool, works for a finance company which sends money abroad to impoverished Third World countries.

I suggested a moment ago that I never had a wife who stayed with me. That was only after three of them. The pattern would recur twice

38 Henry and Edward, Johnny's sons by Cynthia, with his secretary.

more, until I was given the wonderful gift of Janey coming into my life—though I nearly lost her, through my own foolishness. Up to the time I parted from my third countess, I'd always convinced myself that my marriages didn't break up because of other women. But now, as the writing of this book forces me to reassess, I have to face the simple fact that I went off with Carmel when, technically, I was still married to Diana; and I went off with Cynthia when I was still married to Carmel. Perhaps I have never analysed it before.

Come to think of it, in the decade following Cynthia's departure, my lifestyle hardly merits analysis at all. But I stick by what I said on the opening page: By God, I enjoyed it while it lasted!

SEVEN

MY PLAYBOY YEARS

With my family estate gone and my third marriage over, I had, I suppose, a kind of freedom. And I used it to paint a new Rake's Progress, for the late 1950s and the 1960s were, quite simply, My Playboy Years. Though, in truth, the pattern had been laid nearly a decade earlier when, desperate to get away from the unbearable tensions with Carmel, I went off the rails. Was I pushed? Or was it self-motivated? Even I can't really answer that. I only know that I wanted to express and indulge myself, and I didn't give a damn what anyone else thought about it. If adventure was available, I took it.

Back in 1950 it was pretty racy for a white man to be seen out and about with a black lady. So it caused a flurry of raised eyebrows when I went off to Reid's Hotel in Madeira with a stunning West Indian girl named Tessa Prendergast—it was said that she was the model for a cartoonist who drew big-bosomed girls in the *News of the World* every Sunday, though I never did find out the truth of that. But his cartoon girls certainly had the same figure as Tessa.

I knew that taking her away with me would cause a lot of comment, but it didn't worry me very much. We travelled out by flying boat, but it took a long time to get to Madeira because the plane got only as far as Lisbon and then broke down. We had to stay two or three days. I don't speak Portuguese and anyway I found Lisbon a dreary place. Didn't like it at all. We made the time as pleasurable as possible—but you have to talk as well as go to bed!

In Madeira, I don't think you could call the people who were staying at Reid's 'Society', even if they were all in evening dress and dinner jackets. I didn't have a DJ with me, but a suit and tie was quite adequate dress for the place. When we went into dinner, I with an obviously West Indian girl on my arm, there were eyes everywhere. I thought it was fun. I knew a few people by sight, none of them personally, though I didn't care either way. Some of them I recognised as Newmarket trainers—but when it comes to holding up moral standards they aren't generally at the top of the class.

About that time, before I met Tessa, I remember a wonderful

interlude in London when I got to know Eartha Kitt. She was then at the beginning of her career and not well known but so exquisite to look at. The only problem was getting her out of the place where she worked, a nightclub called Churchill's, where she was being paid £5 a week! To begin with, I used to go there several nights in a row, just to watch her. Finally I managed to get introduced to her and after her cabaret, at about 2 o'clock in the morning, took her out to the Orchid Room, which was in the same street as Claridge's.

As we went in I saw a senior officer in the Household Cavalry, whom I knew, with his wife beside him. We sat down at our table, next to them, and as he looked at Eartha he was clearly struggling between envy and disapproval. A couple of nights earlier I'd been in a tatty pick-up joint for hostesses called the Bag of Nails, a far cry from the fashionable Orchid Room. When I stood up to go and have a pee, he followed me. 'Johnny', he said, 'I really don't think you should bring that girl in here'.

'Really!', I replied. 'Well, she's a bloody sight prettier than the black girl I saw you with at the Bag of Nails the other night.'

That shut him up completely.

I'd like to have known Eartha for much longer. But that waiting up until two in the morning to get her out of Churchill's was a bit too much.

A long time later I came back to London from a holiday in Jamaica, having learned that Tessa Prendergast was now running a club in London called the Little Hut. She must have named it after Nancy Mitford's smash-hit comedy of the year we went to Madeira, when Robert Morley and David Tomlinson took London by storm and kept packed houses laughing for months.

I went to the club and met her—and it started all over again. One night she rang a friend in Jamaica who asked her: 'Where are you?'

To which she replied cheerfully: 'I'm in bed with Johnny'.

Oh, she was a sweet girl.

So too was May Maude Redgrave, 'Babs' to her intimates, a dazzlingly glamorous girl to whom I was introduced by Michael Stoop, an old soldier friend—another Grenadier, naturally—who was the greatest womaniser I ever met in my life. He made me look a novice! Babs and I hit it off at once. It was explosive.

When Michael left the Army he went to University College, Oxford. I didn't want to do that. Having left the Army, it would have been like going back to school. But he survived the transition. One day he rang me, asked me down to Oxford for the weekend, and booked me into the Mitre, which is not far from the college. And since it was he who had introduced us, I took Babs along too.

While we were lying in bed on our first morning there she suddenly asked me: 'When are we going to get married?'

I replied: 'I'm sorry, darling, but I still have a wife, which is a minor obstacle'.

'In which case', she said, 'I will marry Sir Dudley Cunliffe-Owen Bt'.

'Bully for you', I responded.

And some years later, she did marry him. Sir Dudley, together with another reprobate called Tim Holland, started the casinos in the Isle of Man. He and I became great friends in later life, and very nearly won the Whitsome Foursomes at golf at Le Touquet. We got as far as the final, but Dudley—who was pissed at the time—had an airshot on the putting green and fell over. He'd been married three times himself, so he didn't worry unduly about my affair years before with Babs.

By the end of the 1950s, the Press was on to me in a big way. Hardly surprising, because at that time and into the Sixties I was single-mindedly set on meeting girls, taking them to dinner and nightclubs and, hopefully, to bed. I have no idea how many women I slept with in those years. I had only to be seen with a new girl in tow, and the gossip columnists were breathing down our necks. Not that I minded altogether—it rather fitted in with the playboy image that I was happily embracing.

When I moved out of Kimberley, leaving Cynthia still in residence, and took a flat in London, I was fair game. So there was inevitably a photographer at the airport when I set off for Paris with blonde, 28-year-old Sandra Renwick, whose marriage to her wealthy, much older husband was breaking up at the same time as mine. There's a picture on file, showing both of us po-faced, and sticking firmly to the line that we were just good friends.

Sandra had business interests in my home county of Norfolk. She set up a club for well-heeled farmers in a handsome house in Hunstanton, looking down on the sea. It didn't last. Farmers preferred staying by their firesides and holding on to their cash, and poor Sandra went bust.

A few months later, both paparazzi (if the word was invented then) and scribblers were at hand again to spotlight two new women in my life. First there was Jane Garnett, dark haired and attractive, with whom I was snapped at a charity ball and a première. 'We are business associates', Jane told them coolly. And we were. For even in the midst of my packed round of socialising and womanising, I was already tentatively moving towards a new career, as one of the first of London's glossy, top-drawer public relations agencies. But more of that later.

My other companion at the night-spots was red haired, curvaceous and very glamorous actress, Yvonne Buckingham, just 21, who had recently promoted herself to the gossip headlines by getting herself registered as a ship at Lloyd's! With me, she navigated the shoals of the West End clubs and restaurants—for a time.

'It's only a week since I first met him', she told the *Daily Mail* breathlessly, 'but we're going out together tonight for the fourth time. I'm very fond of him. He's very sweet—and a frightfully good dancer … I like slim men—and he's very slim. Handsome too'.

Three weeks later the story had changed, as the *Daily Sketch* crowed triumphantly. 'He wanted to take me out to lunch and dinner every day', Yvonne complained. 'But I'm a career girl. I couldn't stand the pace.'

The columnist, however, couldn't resist a bitchy punch-line. 'But perhaps the Earl will be able to fill the vacancy with one of his other friends. Lovely Beverley Roberts, for instance. The Earl has been out and about with her too. She's an old friend of American millionaire Paul Getty—and less talkative than career girl Yvonne.'

A few days later the *Evening Standard* joined the fun. Yvonne was taking part in a publicity event beside a swimming pool, in which it was contractually agreed that she should not get her hair wet. Unfortunately, things went wrong and she, and her hair, were thoroughly dunked, to the consternation of the public relations man for the occasion, Prince Yurka Galitzine. Later, towelled and clutching a whisky, she poured out her woes to the *Standard*, whose columnist observed: 'Her style of delivery is what literary critics used to call the Stream of Consciousness'.

The stream, as he found, was far from exhausted: 'What a day it's been. I'm announcing that I've broken off my friendship with the Earl of Kimberley, by the way. He rang me every day, you know—every day'.

Later, Miss Buckingham and Prince Yurka were sharing the journalist's taxi, when the following conversation ensued:

'Care for a spot of dinner?', asks Galitzine.

'Well, I was going to eat at the corner café', says Miss B.

Minutes afterwards, as the columnist was to record, Yvonne 'is entering a chi-chi club, with damp hair, mourning the loss of an Earl, escorted by a Prince'. And the pity of it was, she and I never got to bed.

Still, if I needed comforting, there was the lure of tobogganing—in the ballroom of the Savoy Hotel, no less. It was the pre-Christmas Cresta Ball, well attended by my old friends of the St Moritz crowd, and intent on having fun, with as centrepiece of the entertainment, a race in which participants settled themselves stomach-down on trays and hand paddled across the dance floor to the finishing line.

There was no cabaret, for as organiser Mrs Vernon Pope explained: 'After seeing your friends down on their tummies, sliding across the floor, a cabaret would be an anti-climax'.

The next year came an equally constructive event, designed to help the great and good pass their time cheerfully, while incidentally raising a fair amount of charitable cash for the National Playing Fields Association. This was the Great Tiddlywinks Championship, held at the Empress Club at the bottom of Berkeley Street, sponsored from afar by Prince Philip (on board HMY *Britannia*), who had his own team captained by a retired full general!

I can't remember who asked me to get involved in the Great Tiddlywinks Championship. Anyway, I bought some winks and a little shaker, and kept them in my pocket. When I went to a restaurant for lunch or dinner, I put the winks on the table and practised flipping them into the wineglasses. Well, if you're going to do something, then you should do it well!

I learned all the rules of tiddlywinks, like squapping and de-squapping. A squap is when you drop your wink on to somebody else's wink, then they can't play their wink because you have covered it. To de-squap, you have to drop another wink onto the two already there, and then you can claim your opponent's winks.

So there we were, sixteen men scrabbling about on the floor of a smart club in Mayfair, encouraged by the banter of a distinguished audience—an all-male stag affair, incidentally, which infuriated heiress Bobo Sigrist no end, because she'd personally coached one of the participants. Cambridge University were defending their reigning champions status.

Prince Philip's team was led by General Sir Hugh Stockwell, who

39 Kevin McLory (left) and Terry-Thomas (centre) with Johnny at the tiddlywinks championship of the world.

was Allied Commander at Suez. My team consisted of Kevin McLory, friend (and winks pupil of Miss Sigrist) and maker of one of the James Bond films; that splendid comedy actor Terry-Thomas; and *Evening Standard* columnist Jeremy Campbell.

The match was introduced by Arthur Dickson Wright, famous then both as a cancer surgeon and as an after-dinner speaker; and more recently revived as father of Clarissa Dickson Wright, the side-car riding half of television's vastly popular *Two Fat Ladies* series.

As a young man Dickson Wright honed his surgical skills in Singapore before settling in London, where he quickly worked his way to the top at St Mary's Hospital, Paddington. A ward there is now named after him. As his reputation grew, so did his client list, which featured film stars like Vivien Leigh, and international royalty, including the Sultana of Jahore. I knew him well, and sympathised with him when in later life he slid into alcoholism—just as I did, but I escaped the demon drink before it was too late.

That night at the Empress Club, 'Dick', as he was known to his friends, was in his usual sparkling public speaking form, and there to hear him was the match's promoter, Sir Vivien Fuchs, the explorer.

'When I woke up this morning and took my bath', declared Dick, 'I lay there wondering how I was going to introduce our promoter and pronounce his name right. However, you may rest assured that Fooks is not the right way to pronounce it. It is a Yorkshire name, and is pronounced as it is spelt, so it is Sir Vivien Fucks … '.

The merriment was completed by a telegram from Prince Philip in *Britannia*: 'I expect the contest to be carried through in the usual thoroughly unsportsmanlike manner'. To his team the message was grim: 'You had better win this time, otherwise I will see to it that your winking licence is withdrawn. Get in there and fight'. But it didn't help. Cambridge won by an embarrassingly large margin.

This was clearly a time for wacky goings on. I was having a holiday break in the south of France and was asked if I'd ever played at bowling. I hadn't. But never being one to pass up an opportunity, I agreed to play—and found myself enrolled in the Grand Monte Carlo International Bowling Competition. Among my memorabilia, I have a cutting of a photo in *Nice Matin* showing me in action—and with the most marvellously Gallic caption which reads: 'Au grand bowling international de Monte Carlo, admirez donc le style de ce gentleman, le très honorable lord John Kimberley, lieutenant des grenadiers de la garde'.

It was a drum roll for a battle of a different kind waiting to explode in London, when I was pitched into the leadership of hundreds of motorists against 'the Parking Prussians'—parking meters and traffic wardens had arrived in the capital. It was not the first, and sadly not the last, of alien American ideas to hit our shores.

The press gleefully waded in to record events as uproar reigned when Westminster residents, used to parking their cars outside their doors, were repeatedly booked by the 'yellow hats', the council was inundated with angry complaints and both the AA and RAC came out fighting on our behalf. The description I coined of 'Parking Prussians' hit the headlines—and so did my tirades against 'these little Hitlers' turning Mayfair into a 'concentration camp' with drivers as the persecuted victims.

That master of his craft, Joseph Lee, produced a classic cartoon in his London Laughs by Lee series in the *Evening News*, with me galloping in, armed to the helm, on a white charger, and my neighbours, bowler hatted and briefcased, mocking police and wardens with Heil Hitler salutes and goose-step marching.

Like all my neighbours, I was furious at traffic meters being

WARDENS-
-PARKERS
WAR

EARL TO FIGHT
'PARKING
PRUSSIANS

" Conduct liable to cause a Breach of the Peace . . ."

40 Johnny fights the traffic wardens.

slapped in without any dialogue with residents—but then, do councils ever consult us? In my case, my South Audley Street flat had a neatly convenient parking spot outside the back door of Thomas Goodes, the famous china shop. Then one night, in came the council squads and put up posts for the new meters. I promptly pulled them out! But the next day the storm-troopers came back and put them in again. I finally accepted the inevitable. My handyman, who lived in, fed the meter for me, at 6d. a time—and was arrested for his trouble.

That was too much. In lordly fury, I summoned the chief inspector from the local police station to attend on me! He did, I said my piece forcefully—and nothing more was heard about the arrest. But parking restrictions and those wretched meters were here to stay, and from London spread nationwide like a plague. It was, you might say, the first stage of that long progression of harassment of motorists, which still goes on remorselessly, by government, local authorities and police.

Soon after these doughty events, I forsook London for a visit to Jamaica, with no thought then that the island would play a crucial role in my life at a time when I was at a dangerously low ebb, and alcohol addiction was in control. Yet this first assay there left me less than impressed. It looked shoddier than I expected—and it rained. As if that wasn't enough, it was a wasted journey.

I'd gone there to seek out a Greek girl named Thana, whose father was Spyros Skouras, one of the Hollywood moguls who owned 20th Century Fox. I'd met Thana on one of her trips to London, and I flew the Atlantic to see her again in hopes of a new liaison. But it didn't happen. It was one of my rare failures, for when I got there, I found that she had a boyfriend already, one of the Americans who owned the hotel where we were both staying.

From the vantage point of my seventies, I look back now over the years and think: 'How much money did I spend, just chasing women?' The truth is, I can't possibly say how much. Fortunately I liked flying. And the caviar was good in those days too. The drawback was that, in comparative terms, it was just about as expensive as it is now to travel first class—which I always did, naturally. But if nothing else, that trip did sow the seeds in my mind of business possibilities in Jamaica, which would ripen in their own good time.

At least, I was back in London in time for millionaire takeover man Charlie Clore's fantastic Derby Night party, when he took over, so to speak, half the Dorchester. At the time he was in the throes of a bid to buy out Watney's brewery. But he still insisted that young Mark Watney should be among his guests.

In the other half of the Dorchester, another party was going on, this one for Harry Carr, the winning jockey, and given by Frank More O'Ferrall, the bloodstock dealer. The two parties merged, with evening-dressed guests taking a short cut via the hotel kitchens, and weaving their way among pots and pans and chefs and waiters.

Ali Khan was there with the delectable Kim Novak on his arm. Among the throng there were, by all accounts, 25 millionaires, including Paul Getty, at that time the richest man in the world, the Greek shipping tycoon Stavros Niarchos and the Maharaja of Jaipur. Among Charlie's personal guests were three ministers of the Crown, two dukes (Argyll and Bedford), two earls (Bessborough and me); and a large bevy of the swish and the rich.

Charlie's circle of friends in high places was legendary. I got on

41 Charles Clore of City Centre Properties.

very well with him, probably because I wasn't a Yes-man. When he bought his 3,000-acre Stype Grange estate, near Hungerford, in Berkshire, he asked me over to shoot there. It was a lovely November afternoon, and at about four o'clock we were walking back to the house together.

'You are a very lucky man', I said to him. 'But on the other hand you have made your luck. We've had a lovely day's shooting, with lots of birds.'

'Well, we haven't got many birds in the house tonight', he replied. 'Will you ring somebody up for me?'

'No, I won't', I snapped. 'I'm not your bloody pimp.'

He never held it against me, not even when, a year or so later, he tried it on with one of my girlfriends whom I'd taken along with me—and she slapped his face.

He was fairly short in stature, but had a lot of personality. A great character, in fact, if a rough-edged one, and a generous host, who in turn was welcomed into the greatest houses in England.

Typical of that generosity was when one of his big business deals kept him longer in the States than he expected. Earl Beatty, Lord Brooke and I, all close friends of his, were due at Stype Grange for a little shooting party. On his instructions his secretary telephoned us: 'Please go ahead with the shoot—My staff will look after you'. Apart from the excellent shooting, Stype Grange maintained a chef and butler, a splendid library and a heated indoor swimming pool. Even without our host, we managed very nicely. Charlie often shot at Blenheim at the invitation of the late Duke of Marlborough, who was known as the Blood Orange because of his reddish, orange looking face, and was renowned as a brilliant shot and notable for the sharp edge of his tongue.

Charlie used to have as his loader the instructor from the Holland & Holland shooting school at Northolt. Clore asked the duke if he might bring his instructor with him into lunch.

'Why?', barked the Blood Orange. 'Do you want him to teach you to eat, as well as shoot?'

The duke's shooting brilliance I can vouch for. The only problem was that he shot at anything that moved, with devastating accuracy, and I remember being rained on by pheasants. Also there that day was Michael Astor. At the end of the shoot Astor came over to thank his host. 'Thank you for a magnificent day's shooting as usual, Bert. Oh, and by the way, would you like to come over and watch me shoot my pheasants next week?'

The Blood Orange's urge not to let anything with feathers escape his marksmanship was topped one day when he committed the dastardly deed of shooting a carrier pigeon. Among the guests standing by as the bird thudded to the ground was David Niven. He enquired politely, in those distinct and polished tones: 'Any mail for me today, Your Grace?'

The Blood Orange never did live in the real world. He went to stay in some smart house but did not find everything to his liking. He came down to breakfast the next morning and told a fellow guest: 'Extraordinary house this. I was given a toothbrush last night with no toothpaste on it'.

Back in the real world, Isaac David Hillman and his wife, a couple who owned a property company (with his wife, according to Hillman, providing the business brain and the cause of his success) which had just made a clear profit of £610,000 in four days—a fair amount of money in the mid 1950s. As a celebratory gesture, they threw a dinner party, with as varied a collection of people round one big, round table as you were likely to find in London.

There were the seriously rich Maharaja and Maharani of Jaipur, gossip columnist Logan Gourlay of the *Daily Express*, myself, and a lady of some note in showbiz and society circles, whom Logan meticulously named as 'Princess Djordjadze, formerly Lady Ashley, formerly Mrs Douglas Fairbanks Snr, formerly Lady Stanley, formerly Mrs Clark Gable, formerly Sylvia Hawkes'. And still not looking old enough to have been married five times. And finally, there was my old friend and prince of property deals, Felix Fenston, escorting Countess Ahlefeldt-Laurig. It must be the only dinner party whose conversation was reported, almost verbatim, a couple of days later in a national newspaper. Though perhaps that was just what bright Mrs Hillman intended.

Felix Fenston enjoyed himself, as well he might, for this characterful man had a quirky, curious sense of humour and a competitive streak with something of the calculation of chess-playing in it. Yet more curiously, he had passed these traits down to his son Timothy. Take the following example.

Felix and Timothy arrived at the airport together to catch the Paris flight. Felix realised he had forgotten his passport, and suggested to the passport desk that, as his son was with him, the young man could confirm his identity. When asked to do so by the officer on duty,

42 Susan and Michael Wilding with Johnny at the Savoy, Christmas 1959.

Timothy looked at his father and replied: 'Never seen the man in my life before', and went through to the aircraft, leaving his father to return home, collect his passport, and catch the next available plane.

Before Felix left the house, however, he phoned an old friend at Scotland Yard and requested a little help, so that he might have a subtle revenge. His contact told the French authorities that a young man on a certain flight was travelling on a stolen passport, and should be arrested. And indeed Timothy was arrested, and hauled off to be put in a police station cell, where he stayed until his father arrived, gloating triumphantly, to rescue him.

I ended 1959, still with the loss of Kimberley keen in my mind, and mindful too that I was now in a new world, where I had to apply myself to things practical and do a useful job of work. A push in that direction came in unlikely circumstances. I was frequently escorting a beautiful, highly intelligent, 28-year-old Australian girl named Elizabeth Campbell—who was also said to be very rich. The newspapers claimed that she was an heiress who owned '1,000,000 sheep, £1,000,000, 20 diamond necklaces, 10 diamond bracelets, half a dozen minks, 100 dresses and 85 pairs of shoes'.

She told me this was nonsense. 'If you reduce the figures by more than half, you get nearer to the truth', she assured me. 'Anyway, nobody has 20 diamond necklaces. Still, I'm reasonably rich.'

That didn't mean she wasn't a working woman. So in London she set up a business as an agency for the rich, providing everything from plush flats to trimmed poodles. 'I'm the first member of my family since my grandfather even to think about work', she declared. 'It's not that I want to make a fortune. I just want to do something interesting and amusing.'

When she spoke to the *Daily Express*, however, the line had hardened a little. 'Everybody has to try to do something, however unimportant', she declared. 'The days of the idle, privileged rich are over. In another age, people like Johnny Kimberley and myself wouldn't have been expected to do anything. But we have to adjust ourselves to 1959.' So be it. And for me the wheels were already in motion. But that didn't mean I was going to stop enjoying myself.

It was a lunch invitation from Logan (Jack) Gourlay of the *Daily Express* which gave the first push. Jack was the Beaver's favourite journalist, and though he was bone idle he could get away with anything in Beaverbrook's eyes. Jack gave me a bloody good lunch at Les Ambassadeurs and wrote an article with the eye-catching headline—Rich Young Aristocrat Looking for Work!

I had many calls, among them one from George Dawson, the most famous junk and scrap metal man of the 1950s and early Sixties, a big, thick-set fellow and a great character. He told me that I should buy a destroyer, which he knew of, secondhand, from the Navy, take it to Spain, load it up with cheap nutty slack and bring it back to England. 'With my brains and your money we could do anything', he carolled. Even with such a carrot, it was an offer I didn't take up.

At that time I encountered two other notable characters, Raemonde and Dora Rahvis, two tough Jewish sisters, both ugly as sin, but very clever and kind, who ran a haute couture salon in Brooke Street, where Raemonde had a lovely apartment over the shop.

They had a cocktail party one evening, to which I was invited.

'I want to talk to you when everyone has gone', said Raemonde.

I looked at her and wondered: 'If I have to, could I?'

But it wasn't a proposition. It was a business project.

'You can't continue aimlessly as you have these past months', she advised. 'You should go into public relations.'

I had never even heard of public relations. She suggested I contact Freddy Mullaly and David Wynne Morgan. They ran an office in Davies Street, about three or four doors away from the Davies Street entrance to Claridge's. It was also Freddy's flat. So they met me, we liked each other and I went to work for them on a commission basis. One day they asked a girl to join the company and I at once found her rather attractive. Nature took its course and I had an affair with her. It was she who suggested that I create my own company.

But I need a partner, I said. She suggested Michael Forster, who worked in the movie business as a film publicist. Among his credits were huge successes like *Inn of the Sixth Happiness*, starring Ingrid Bergman; and *Shake Hands with the Devil*, originally called *The Night Fighters*, which was made at studios just outside Dublin. All this meant he had access to film studios and knew a lot of people in show business. An ideal partner, in fact. So it happened, and John Kimberley Associates was launched.

EIGHT

JOHN KIMBERLEY ASSOCIATES

Shortly after forming my public relations company, John Kimberley Associates, I bought a short leasehold on a house in South Audley Street, where I had the office. It had a very nice large drawing room on the first floor, which was immediately over the showroom of Thomas Goode & Co., London's leading china shop, which made a very good room for entertaining potential and current clients. My partner, Michael Forster, and myself had a few people to drinks one evening, mostly from show business, like Robert Mitchum, Stewart Granger, Gina Lollobrigida, and some others in big business. At that time I employed a Chinaman who happened to be called Kim. One day Forster and I decided to have lunch at home, because Kim said he was a very good cook. We asked for lunch at 1 p.m. and finally had it at 3 p.m., by which time we were both pissed and I realised that Chinese time is different from English. On the night of the party, Kim was doing drinks, which he was very good at. As the drawing room was on the first floor, people had to walk up a flight of stairs or, on leaving, go down. At one stage I went into the room next door, which was the dining room, to order some more drinks and I saw Kim standing at the bottom of the staircase seeing his boyfriend out, with the lights on and the front door wide open, stark bollock naked! I gave myself a large whisky and retired back to the drawing room. Then some of the lady guests started to leave and before I could do anything, they proceeded to walk downstairs. One or two of them actually shook the Chinaman's 'dong' by the hand as they walked past. As I said, the door was wide open, so no-one walking past could fail to see this apparition standing naked in my front hall and I wondered what the gossip would be about my strange habits! So the next day I had to fire Kim. He asked if it was anything to do with his behaviour the previous night and I said 'No, nothing at all—it is because you are so unpunctual!'

So that was a great start to my public relations career!

Camden Town at the turn of the 1960s may have seemed a strange place for a fashionable public relations outfit to stage its first big

43 Michael Forster and girlfriend.

promotion. But it worked for us, because our venue was the head office of Gilbeys—and through them we were launching Smirnoff Vodka in London, and aiming to promote vodka drinking in Britain. Vodka was quaffed, and caviar downed almost as quickly (Gilbey's were footing the bill) by a circle of glitterati who had come at my behest. Among them were the Duchess of Argyll, actors Michael Denison and his wife Dulcie Gray, Woodrow Wyatt MP, and Norman Hartnell, the Queen's dressmaker.

We asked our guests to come up with new vodka cocktails. Socialite Mrs Bunty Kinsman, wife of a Lloyd's underwriter, spirited up a 'recipe' which earned her a roar of approval. She called it 'Deb's Downfall': Add five parts of vodka to five parts of vodka. Mingle a bitter tear. Then share it with a Siberian wolf.

With my reputation, it was probably a highly appropriate launcher for John Kimberley Associates.

Interestingly, despite all my efforts, the Savoy, the Connaught and Claridge's, all in the same group, declined to take Smirnoff. I never did discover why. Still, the vodka promotion worked well, and Gilbeys were happy. A very different story from one of my original (and admittedly, amateurish) forays into the craft of PR, when I thought I could make a penny and do my old friend Matthew Banks a favour.

Matty was the Australian doctor and plastic surgeon who taught me to fly his Auster light aircraft, and flew me over to the Isle of Wight to stay with Pat Aitken—and to meet her sister Carmel. Also he often flew us over to Paris for some fun weekends—and competed against me in our road v. air race when I beat his Auster to Newmarket in my brilliant Healey car.

So it was that one day I asked him if he'd employ me as his PR man.

'Well', he said, 'McIndoe' (Sir Archie, the great pioneer of plastic surgery during the war) 'has someone working for him'.

'Fine', I said. 'So what are you going to be doing in the next week or so that's newsworthy?'

Matty replied that he was going to fly to Israel to do free plastic surgery on Israeli children.

Noble charity work, and with children! Couldn't be better. I arranged for a *Daily Mail* reporter I knew to go and interview him. But there was a skeleton in Matty's cupboard which I didn't know about and the *Mail* did. A year earlier he'd been caught smuggling gold bars out of Croydon and fined £500. This was added to the story, and of course he was livid, and blamed it all on me. So that was the first PR job that I 'blew', though really it wasn't my fault.

There was a man in the rag trade, Jack Saville, who owned Saville Sportswear, next door to Hartnell's Royal Dorchester. He sold at quite good prices, but he did sell rubbish. I persuaded him to put on a show each year with models parading up and down the catwalk. I also employed a Society girl named Anne Lambton (for a time the wife of Edward Lambton, the highly respected Newmarket racehorse trainer) who knew a lot about fashion, and looked after the female dress side of the business.

Days later we had a very good write-up in the *News of the World*—which pleased Jack not at all. As far as he was concerned, it was a vulgar, dirt-digging paper of which he strongly disapproved. I made Jack understand that it had the biggest circulation of any London newspaper, and that was what counted. The businessman in him saw the point, as businessmen will when it comes to a choice between profit and scruples.

Once we had John Kimberley Associates in operation, right from the start Michael Forster and I were aiming high. Our first big international push was a month-long round tour of the USA, promoting our new company and drumming up a healthy client list. We covered New York, Los Angeles, Hollywood, Dallas, back to New

York, then returned to England. It was a terrific success and the big names, in both showbiz and business, rolled in. It was hard work—but still as easy as falling off a log. And the Americans loved the 'belted Earl' bit.

It was in New York that someone asked me if I'd like to meet Burl Ives. I said I would, very much. So arrangements were made and one afternoon I and two or three others were invited up to his house. He was propped up in an enormous bed, surrounded by a bevy of beautiful girls, with a bottle of whisky beside him—and was playing his guitar. He had an incredible repertoire of songs, mostly lewd, but very, very funny. In between songs he slugged the entire bottle of Scotch while I was there. It proved to be one of the most entertaining afternoons I've ever had.

With my love of big band music, I had the pleasure in Los Angeles of meeting Stan Kenton, the band leader, who was playing in a nightclub called the Crescendo. I was there night after night to listen to him, and to sit by the piano and talk to him. Michael couldn't stand the music. In fact he wasn't musical at all. Kenton was charming, educated and polite. I adored his music, and still do.

Michael and I then flew on to Dallas. On our third night there we went to a pretty crummy nightclub belonging to Jack Ruby, the man who shot Lee Harvey Oswald, John F. Kennedy's assassin.

In Texas you can't buy drink in a club. You take your own and they serve you minerals. Michael took whisky, and I chose vodka. We both got pissed, though he was in a worse condition than I was. The floorshow was dreadful, a lousy striptease act. We'd soon had enough and I asked for the bill. It was a very big one, and we looked at it in disbelief. But we paid and left smartly—after a huge creature hovered over us, like an outsize evil genie, and enquired menacingly: 'Anythin' wrong with yo' bill, gen'el'men?'

On the PR front, our track record showed that we hadn't been wasting our time in between the socialising. The *Kinematograph Weekly*—no doubt impressed by the fact that we were already promoting all the smash-hit films in London, from *Ben Hur* to *El Cid*, and had companies like 20th Century Fox among our clients and top films publicist Arthur Jacobs among our personal pals—was recording our progress:

> John Kimberley Associates is already representing many of the
> biggest names in show business, in addition to a number of

industrial accounts. On a reciprocal basis it has been appointed representative in Great Britain of the Arthur P. Jacobs Organisation of New York, Hollywood, Paris and Rome; and will handle Deborah Kerr, Gina Lollobrigida, Yul Brinner, Henry Fonda, James Stewart, Van Johnson, Bette Davies, Gregory Peck, Joseph Mankiewicz, Eve Marie Saint, Jean Simmons, Hubble Robinson Productions, Lerner & Loewe and the Ed Sullivan Show. Also through the Jacobs organisation it will look after the interests in this country of Prince Rainier and Princess Grace of Monaco.

The list was nearly right. But no, we didn't represent the Rainiers. The prince and I were at prep school together. When my father was killed during the war, Rainier heard about it and sent me a letter of commiseration. The next time I went to southern France after the war I wrote to him to say I would like to thank him personally for his thoughtfulness. But an aide at the palace told me: 'He's never heard of you!'. I suggested he might remember me from schooldays as Wodehouse, rather than Kimberley. No response.

I rang the palace, but to no avail. I wrote again, this time addressing him, not as 'Dear Rainier', as in my first letter, but as 'Your Serene Highness', hoping that might please him. But answer came there none. So I never did meet him—or represent him and Princess Grace in Britain.

And the stars? I met many of them. La Lollo wasn't very intelligent, but buxom and pretty and easy to get on with. I took her to Fortnum & Mason and got her to buy a whole Stilton cheese, with the manager there in his penguin suit. The picture got into all the papers. Robert Mitchum was a lovely man, Gregory Peck enchanting, but a bore.

When he and David Niven were over here making *The Guns of Navarone*, and publicising the film, they wanted to go to Ascot, and I managed to arrange it for them. Gregory went off to Savile Row and had a magnificent morning suit made for himself. Being a tall, big man he looked superb. But David Niven went to Moss Bros and hired a suit. You would have thought that with Niven being so slim and elegant, it would have been easy to fit him. But it didn't fit him anywhere, and looked dreadful.

I took them down in a chauffeur-driven car, together with David's Swedish wife, Hjördis. In case they should get parted in the crowd,

David told her to be at the champagne bar after the third race. When she wasn't, he got very cross, and really set about her when she eventually reappeared.

Gregory Peck was delightfully easy to get along with, and at the races was in his element, because he loved horses, having some of his own in America. He gave me a gramophone record, of the twist, which had only just arrived in Britain. A girl named Sandu Scott had brought it to London, where she was including it in her cabaret act at the Colony Restaurant in Berkeley Square. She was a very, very sexy looking blonde Canadian, whom I got to know and liked a lot. I introduced her to Charlie Clore, and they had what was for a time a very happy affair.

Charlie had a chauffeur-butler-manservant, Kay, upon whom he relied completely. Each Saturday night it was Kay's job to drive up to London to pick up Sandu at the Colony at the end of her act at midnight, and drive her down to Stype Grange. I heard him talking to one of his mates, saying he wished the bloody girl had never brought the twist to England, because the Saturday night drive was such a bind. But she'd told me how happy she was with Charlie, and I'd told her how glad I was that they got on well together.

Just before Christmas, the axe dropped and she rang me in tears. 'Charlie says I can't go down to the house for Christmas, though he's already invited me.'

I telephoned him and said: 'You're a rude little sod. I always thought you were.'

Pretty shamefacedly, he replied: 'I didn't think it would be very good with my children if I had the girl down here at Christmastime.'

'You've broken her heart', I told him. 'You're a little shit.' It was a dirty trick. He'd had her down there at weekends and for a day's shooting. Why couldn't he have her with him at Christmas? I think that was the end of the affair between them. And anyway, London got bored with the twist.

But Sandu was a survivor, and had sensibly put a little by for a rainy day. When she first arrived, this lithe, vivacious girl was pursued by what the gossip columnists described as 'a dazzle of princes', including the energetic Prince Christian of Denmark. She'd also laid by a tidy collection of diamonds and four mink stoles, admitting coyly: 'I like money and the things it can buy'. To which she added sadly: 'At the moment I'm fresh out of princes. Maybe I'll meet another soon'. That must have been about the time that I introduced her to Charlie Clore.

No sooner were Michael Forster and I back from our month in the States than copies arrived on our heels of the *New York Telegraph & Sun* and the *New York Mirror*. The first reported that I was on the point of returning immediately to the States 'and he will take up where he left off in his rather speedy courtship with Joanne Thompson, widow of the millionaire Alexis Thompson'. Wrong! Alexis had been a very fine bobsleigh driver, which was how I met him and as a result was introduced to Joanne.

While I was in New York, I looked her up and she and I had a few days together. It was nothing serious, just a pleasant interlude. What happened to her subsequently I don't know. But if the *Telegraph & Sun* was awry in its facts, Suzi and her Society Column in the *Mirror* were way out, with a story with a few grains of fact in it, and much highly entertaining invention.

I had, she informed her readers, stepped from the plane at London Airport on return from the States wearing a ten-gallon white stetson which I'd bought in Dallas. 'He is mad about the hat actually and hopes his English buddies feel the same way. If they don't, that's tough! He is going to wear it anyhow, even to Ascot.'

However, revealed the inventive Suzi, we'd been most impressed by our visit to a Japanese psychiatrist at her house up in the Hollywood Hills where, it seems, we'd arrived three hours late (having lost our way *en route*). We needed Martinis badly (true!) but Chico-Chico-San didn't get the message. Instead she called in her horse-sized Alsatian, which arrived with a budgerigar perched on its head and a Siamese cat in its mouth (that's true too).

'Ashen faced', Suzi assured her gripped audience, 'the two English gentlemen fled'. The fact is, we fled for a drink, for which we were gasping, and went straight to the nearest watering hole.

It was soon after our American tour that Cynthia, my third countess, was granted a decree nisi in the divorce court 'because of adultery by the Earl of Kimberley with an unknown woman at a Chelsea flat last May'. With my track record, the press gossips followed me like hounds, and in no time at all were not only forecasting another marriage for me, but detailing who the lucky lady would be.

'If precedent is any guide, the Earl of Kimberley, aged 36 and with three marriages behind him, will not stay single long', trumpeted the *Express*. 'When his first two marriages were dissolved, he wed again in the following year ... His friends expect him to run true to form.'

The girl they'd pinpointed for me was Roberta Kirkwood, 27-year-old ex-debutante and daughter of Sir Robert Kirkwood, chairman of the Jamaica Sugar Manufacturers Association, and head of Tate & Lyle. Certainly I knew her well, had escorted her several times and, as the newspaper artfully added: 'Recently Lord Kimberley was the guest of the Kirkwoods at their Jamaica home'.

Roberta asked me to come out and stay. She met me at the airport at Kingston, and I noticed at once that she was wearing a big engagement ring.

'Roberta', I said, 'I didn't know, darling, that you were engaged, or I wouldn't have come'.

She admitted that she had in fact bought the ring herself, and had announced to all white society in Jamaica that she was engaged to be married to me.

'That's a bit awkward', I said, 'because I've still got a wife'.

Unfortunately we didn't get on very well. Her father too was very difficult. We played bridge every night, and every night he reduced his wife to tears at the bridge table. He was not a nice man, Sir Robert. Subsequently Roberta married Major Nicholas Collins, 'Nick' to his friends, a racehorse owner, and director of the Anglo-Irish Agency, one of the world's largest bloodstock businesses.

While dallying with upper crust girls like Roberta could have its very pleasurable side, a spot of assignation has its own excitements. Take an occasion when I was already slumming it a bit by staying in the Guards Club dormitory. It had about six beds in it, and cost just 5s. a bed. At around 4 o'clock in the morning its clients might be found struggling back in, having been to some pick-up joint, and dossing down for the rest of the night.

I'd arranged to meet a girl at the Grosvenor House Hotel, where she was staying, and take her out to dinner and afterwards to a nightclub. We had a good evening together, got on very well, and eventually headed back towards her hotel.

'I've only got a single room', she said.

'That doesn't matter', I replied.

She was smartly dressed. I was in a tuxedo. Knowing that the hotel would disapprove of unofficial 'co-habiting', I said: 'We'll walk straight past reception and straight into the lift. I'll go one floor higher than your room, and then walk down the stairs'. This we did, and minutes later, we were together in our little love-nest and lost no time in getting into bed.

Twenty minutes later there was a thumping on the door and a male voice growled: 'Come out of there. I know you're in there'.

Before he'd opened the door and stepped in, I'd stowed away in the wardrobe—stark naked. He came in, looked around and (wise from previous experience, no doubt) headed straight for the wardrobe and opened it.

He looked at me, world wearily, and said: 'You can't stay 'ere'.

'Right', I said. 'But I want a suite.'

'Then you'll have to do that from reception.'

I rang reception, told them I wanted a suite immediately, and promptly was advised that I couldn't arrange that over the phone and would have to come downstairs.

You feel rather vulnerable when you are caught by a house-dick and you're stark naked. He certainly had the advantage of me. I dressed quickly and went down to reception. Unfortunately I had no money on me at all, because normally I signed at restaurants and nightclubs, working on the principle that if I had no cash, I couldn't get 'rolled'. But I did have the gold cigarette case, given to me by the Kimberley tenants when I returned home after the war. This I produced, but they refused to accept it. They did, however, accept a cheque.

'You must be daft', I told them.

They gave me a blank cheque, and I filled it in. By that time it was around 5 a.m. and nearly daylight, and the romance of several hours earlier had decidedly flopped, in more senses than one.

The girl for whom I'd gone through all these hopes was Hungarian, and as beautiful and exotic as Magyars can be. When we parted company, she was due to go off to Capri, and I was attracted enough by her to follow her without delay, so anxious was I to see her again. And that's what I did.

When I arrived, I rang her, only to find she was already shacked up with another lover. So that was another wasted woman-chasing trip. Still, I came back via the South of France, looked up an old girl friend there, and passed in her company, and bed, a lovely and satisfying fortnight. Whereupon I returned to London.

Then Maggie came into my life.

NINE

MAGGIE, ASPINALL AND OTHERS

Margaret Simons, model and small-time actress, very beautiful, stunningly so, with a wonderful figure you couldn't better today. And she had a brain and was witty. I thought she was the most beautiful looking female creature I had ever seen. She laughed at my jokes too. Unutterably corny as it may seem, that Rodgers & Hammerstein song from *Oklahoma!* was trilling in my mind—'Don't laugh at my jokes too much—People will say we're in love'. And we were, head over heels, each with the other.

Already I'd seen her many times, but didn't know her. I met her at one of the many booze parties I went to in London in those days. I'd seen her around, because she used to be a girlfriend of Paul Adam, who was very much the Society band leader of the time. She shared a flat with another actress, Sue Lloyd, who looked like Kay Kendall, and had been in the television series *Crossroads*. She played, I think, the manageress of the motel where the action was set.

Despite a lot of phone calls and a lot of trying, Maggie still firmly said 'No' to my urging that she should come out to dinner with me.

'But why not?' I asked.

'Because all you want is to go to bed with me', she replied.

'Why not?' I rejoined.

At last she agreed to dinner, and we had a super evening together. The next evening she had dinner with me again.

Things developed rather rapidly. We went out to nightclubs and restaurants together and I was more and more taken with her. But she still wouldn't go to bed with me. A week after our first meeting, I proposed to her. She was completely taken by surprise.

'Are you serious?' she asked.

'Yes, I am.'

'All right, then I will.' That night I was given my reward, for as she put it: 'If I'm going to marry you, then I'd better go to bed with you.'

Only three or four days later, we were married at Chelsea Register Office. It all seemed to me quite a rational thing to do. Maybe I

44 Maggie, Johnny's fourth wife.

thought the routes to wedded bliss I had been on so far were not attractive. Perhaps I wanted to try a new direction. In any event, I never regretted it.

I was still living in South Audley Street, where my PR company was based. Maggie's flat was 400 yards up the road in Grosvenor Square. After our honeymoon in the South of France (peremptorily cut short by a work commitment in London for another character in my story, John Mills), she joined me in South Audley Street.

Before she met me, Maggie had never touched my kind of life. But now we led a very social life in town and country. We bought a cottage by the Thames at Sonning, near Reading. It was delightful, except that the sun never seemed to shine and every weekend we spent there was accompanied by grey skies and rain.

Maggie came up with me to York where I shot with my old friend Felix Fenston, the property man. To begin with, Maggie hated the idea of killing things, but then I taught her to shoot, and she became remarkably good at it. I bought her a small car—and she promptly ran it into a lamp post in St John's Wood, doing much more damage to the car than to the lamp post. But I still let her drive my Bentley Continental, with L-plates up before she passed her test. There's love for you!

We went to theatres, cinemas and restaurants together, and for both of us it was still a love affair. But I still couldn't help myself, because if I saw a pretty girl across the restaurant I would ask a waiter to get her name for me—while sitting at my table with one of the most beautiful girls in London, with a fantastic figure and lots of it, and which didn't need support anywhere. What's more, she was my wife.

We didn't go abroad much, but when we were invited to Jamaica by a wealthy acquaintance and his wife, to stay in their lovely beach house, Maggie adored it, as I did too, because we were so happy together. Admittedly, though I did stay faithful to Maggie at that period, I couldn't help my roving eyes taking in the cavalcades of lovely girls on the island, and thinking to myself: I should come back here in a couple of years' time.

Our married contentment lasted nearly three years. Then, true to character, I started to stray again. I don't know what went wrong. I remember I was drinking a lot. Possibly we had a row and I just sugared off to a girl who attracted me. There a series of encounters, just passing ships in the night—or two or three nights at most; just physical, meaning nothing.

I had a business partnership with a man called Walter Jokel, who was a theatrical agent. In his photo files he always had a stream of starlets and budding actresses, and of course for me they were bibles of temptation, temptation to which I all too often gave way.

Maggie knew what was going on and she couldn't, and wouldn't,

45 Johnny eating cactus in Marbella.

accept it. A point came where her patience snapped.

Out of the blue, she served divorce papers on me. I was amazed. She had every right to do what she did, but that didn't help me. It had always been me who had done the serving before. I was in the habit of giving, not taking. It was a lesson I had to learn, but at the same time I was furious that a woman could do it to me. I admit it was a blow to my male ego. But I certainly wasn't going to defend it or fight it.

I look back and I think: what a male chauvinist pig I was. In a way, the writing of this book has been a cleansing of my soul for me. It has made me realise what a real shit I have been all my life.

On the night of the day I received the divorce papers, I met some people for drinks at a cocktail party. I told them what had happened, and turned it into a joke in an effort to brazen it out. But inside I was upset, hurt, cross, even though I knew Maggie had every good reason for her actions. I just didn't think she would do it to me.

When we met and married, Maggie was in love with me, not with what I was. We were very, very happy—until I blew it. When the break came, I did have a fear of what lay ahead. There was uncertainty, doubt. I needed someone. I needed a roof. And I knew the sands were running out. I was 41 when the marriage ended, and I knew I had reached a crossroads.

I thought to myself: I have got to get it right before I am 50, because after 50 I am going to be old.

Even with the drinking problem which was already dogging me—the culmination of years of downing booze as if there was no tomorrow—I was confident that at 41 I was still young enough to go off and start a new life. But I knew equally that in ten years' time I would be too old to do so. Yet still, even with this weight of evidence before me, I didn't, essentially, change my ways. The drinking continued on its inevitable path. And my taste for gambling, not only on the horses, but even more so at the tables, took deeper hold.

Despite these preoccupations, work had to go on, for keeping John Kimberley Associates successful and profitable was a major consideration. That meant working at all hours—and dealing, patiently, with the oddest requests. A hotel company in America wrote to me asking if I would find them a typical English pub to install in their hotel. Somebody else contacted me from California with a straightforward query: 'We want to build a Burlington Arcade in Los Angeles. Can you help?' Of course we could help—for a nice, comfortable fee.

46 Johnny with lady friend on Elba.

47 Mrs Michael Stoop (Beverley).

When Bob Hope was over here making a picture, a firm from San Francisco wrote to me, asking if I would finalise a deal in which Bob would do an advertisement for Hiho Sunshine Crackers and Royal Crown Cola. Mr Hope, they assured me, had already agreed and all I needed to do was to contact him. If fact, for reasons I can't recall, the deal never came off. But I'd already received 44 crates of Hiho Sunshine Crackers and 24 dozen bottles of Royal Crown Cola. For many months they sat, disconsolately, untasted and untried, until finally they were dumped.

If work didn't necessarily always come first, it was always near the head of the list, as Maggie learned from the start of our marriage. As I mentioned earlier, we had to come back early from our honeymoon to deal with some business on behalf of one John Mills.

This wasn't his real name, for he hailed from some unnamed backwater in eastern Europe. I first encountered him towards the end of the war, when he opened a restaurant in London called the Milroy, which he'd opened within less than a couple of years of arriving in London from Poland in 1942. I had dinner there on VJ night, fresh back from action in Germany and still in battledress. Suddenly there was a commotion at the door. There was Sonny (Marquess of)

48 John Mills, a nightclub owner.

Blandford, later the Duke of Marlborough, resplendent in evening Blues uniform, giving the head waiter hell because there wasn't a table available for him!

Mills was a bit of a shady character. I never knew where his financial resources came from, even though I worked for him for a short time. Way before that point came, I had dinner with him one night in Monte Carlo. Later we headed back for our hotels, he and his long-time girlfriend in the front, me in the back of his very smart open-top sports car.

Over dinner he and the girl had been having a row.

Suddenly he stopped the car and snarled at her: 'Get out, you bitch'.

She had about 1½ miles to walk back. Even though it was a warm evening, it was hardly a nice thing to do to a lady. Being in the back of a sports car, I couldn't get out. But I called out to Mills: 'Look, you can't do that'.

'You mind your bloody business', he shouted in reply.

As he was about 6 ft 4 in. and built like old Field Marshal Ironside, I decided he could well pick me and throw me over the Corniche, had he wanted to do so. So I shut up! He really was a very nasty individual.

He owned the Metropole Hotel in Monte Carlo, a smart establishment beside the Hôtel de Paris. I stayed there once when I was down

49 Maggie with Charles, Johnny's youngest son.

there having a gambling frolic.

One night at the casino I won £100 in francs, which was better than a kick in the teeth. To celebrate, I downed a few drinks and returned to the hotel, nicely mellowed. I had on a blue dinner jacket,

50 Tiger (the wife that got away), Roberta Saville and Johnny in Jamaica.

made by my tailor in London, quite smart, elegant in fact. By the time I reached the Metropole, the drink had worked on me nicely—so I decided I was Christ Almighty and could walk on water, and duly stepped into the hotel swimming pool. Of course I sank, elegant DJ, money and all, and the following day the francs had to be dried and ironed out!

The job which, a few years later, brought me back to London, still warm from my honeymoon, was the opening of Mills's new casino. It was called Le Cercle, and housed within Les Ambassadeurs club & restaurant (Les-A, to its habitués), in Hamilton Place—and was open only to Ambassadeurs members. Very exclusive! Complete too, with French croupiers, the correct kidney-shape tables, Paris-made chips and all the other accoutrements of a casino. What helped make it a real magnet was that it was the first legal casino in Britain.

There was one big drawback, however—the only game to be played was *chemin-de-fer*, which *The Times* promptly dubbed as 'one of the most expensive and unskilful games in the world'.

Still, the gaming salon was superb, a high-ceilinged, elegant room, hung with tapestries, within a fine town house built in the late 1860s by Baron Leopold Rothschild for his Italian wife. Mills hired me to be his PRO, for which I agreed the ridiculously low initial fee of £500, and I threw myself into it with gusto. Part of my contract was that I was not allowed to gamble in Le Cercle—a very good deterrent for an individual like me.

Before I took on the job several friends had tried to warn me off, pointing out that Mills had treated earlier employees shabbily and refused to pay up what he owed them.

'Oh no, he wouldn't do that to me', I responded.

But he bloody well did. When the time came to pay me, after I'd smoothed the way for his casino, getting the right people in and charming the Press, he declined to cough up.

His reasoning? 'I don't need you any more.'

Months later I was back at Le Cercle, got a bit pissed and told myself: fuck this, if he won't pay me, I'll break our contract too, and gamble. I asked for £500 worth of chips. I wish I could say I won £1,000. I didn't. On the contrary, I lost £500. But I never did pay Mills, so in a way we were quits. Nasty rat that he was, he tried hard to get my money out of me, even through the lawyers. I seem to remember that eventually Mills crashed, though I can't recall how or why.

I still have, tucked away among my memorabilia, a little memento of that time. On the night Le Cercle opened, I played against Mills in the first legal hand in a casino in Britain—and won a bottle of champagne. And I have, neatly framed, a little certificate to prove it.

As time progressed towards the mid Sixties, losing £500 of somebody else's money was a mere detail in my gambling career.

There was a funny little man called Kim Waterfield who used to run small, private *chemin-de-fer* parties in London, which at that time were illegal. If you ran these gatherings you couldn't lose, because you took five per cent for the house out of every winning bet. It might not seem a lot, but five per cent of £10,000 is £500! All you had to do was provide space for nine players (the game doesn't work well with less), some booze and a bit of smoked salmon.

It was money for old rope, provided you didn't get raided by the police. That is why these parties moved from flat to flat each time, with Waterfield paying £100 for the use of the flat.

I once went to the biggest chemmy party ever held outside a casino, and given by John Aspinall, the zoo owner and confidant of the long-vanished Lord Lucan. John, or Aspers, as all of us knew him, died aged 74 in June 2000 from cancer of the jaw, and as everyone expected of him, he went with courage and dignity.

He was a remarkable character by any measure, for whom the

gambling world, from which he made millions, was merely a means to an end—to maintain his zoos and his beloved animals.

I think it was towards the end of the 1950s that he bought his Kent estate, Howletts, with £6,000 he'd won gambling on a race. It became his celebrated Zoo Park, which he extended in the Seventies by including the Port Lympne Zoo.

Against almost solid 'expert' opinion, he achieved astounding results with rare species which had seldom, if ever before, been bred in captivity. Under his care and almost magical gifts with animals, they began to produce offspring regularly.

But it was gorillas with which he had the closest rapport. They were, quite simply, his personal friends. He understood their ordered, family lives, and how they ticked.

Paul Johnson wrote a fine tribute piece to Aspers, which appeared in the *Daily Mail* the day after his death, in which he told an Aspers tale of the day he and his gorillas received a visit from Mrs Thatcher. The Iron Lady produced a bunch of magnificent grapes, and insisted on handing it to one of the female gorillas. 'Ladies first', she said decisively.

The female promptly presented the bunch to the head male gorilla, who meticulously picked the best, then tossed the rest to the females. Mrs Thatcher turned on the male and observed witheringly:

'Well, I think your behaviour is perfectly disgusting.'

Aspers, who had observed this scene with glee, was later to say: 'It was the first and only time I have seen a gorilla blush'.

In one crisp paragraph, Paul Johnson warmly summed up the Aspinall phenomenon: 'He was not a zoologist, an animal behaviourist, a biologist or a trained expert on the environment. He was simply a man who loved wild animals and they loved him'.

It was at Oxford as an undergraduate that he started organising chemmy parties, and realised it was easy money. He gave the huge party, which I have just mentioned, in a private house near Sunningdale, on Gold Cup night at Ascot. There were two tables, a big one and a small one. I played at the small one where you could start a bank for £100. For the big table, he had made some special chips or plaques, each worth £10,000, and it was £10,000 minimum to open a bank. Aspinall took five per cent of every winning bank.

With a bank one can double in value. I worked it out that a chemmy shoe lasts 35 or 40 minutes, and that that shoe will produce probably 15 winning banks. As the game lasted roughly from 11 p.m.

to 10 a.m. the next morning, in that eleven-hour period Aspinall must have netted £200,000 or thereabouts, tax free.

That was the money with which he bought the Clermont Club, the place where Lord Lucan was last seen alive, before he fled following the murder of his family's nanny. At the Clermont, backgammon was my game (taught me by my mother when I was a boy, as I've related in an earlier chapter), and I became pretty good at it.

I used to enter the regular Tuesday night tournaments there, and knew Johnnie Lucan, though he wasn't a friend of mine. In fact on one occasion he was extremely rude to me. Then he disappeared without trace, and I was never able to tell him what a rude sod he was.

But to return to Sunningdale and the chemmy. I won about £150 that evening. As it happened, I owed Bill Stirling, a great friend and a serious gambler, around £75 which I'd borrowed from him in Le Touquet the weekend before. He waved it away. Not surprisingly, it was hardly worth considering, because that night he was on the way to a staggering loss of £100,000.

He was a rich man, but to meet his gambling debt he was forced nonetheless to sell his gorgeous Keir Estate, near Stirling in Scotland. It had everything—grouse moors, duck flighting, deer forests, though I don't think there was a salmon river.

Not long before this calamity, Bill had invited me up to Keir for a few days to a shoot. It was the kind of invitation I would normally leap at with enthusiasm. But as I was due to leave for Jamaica immediately after the shoot, I declined with regret, so I could have an extra couple of days to get ready and packed. Bill rang me and said: 'It's OK, I've booked you on the Glasgow–London flight on the Tuesday evening, to get you back to London at 10 p.m.'. I still decided I wanted more time, and stuck to my original schedule.

The BEA Vanguard on to which he'd booked me ran into fog coming down on to the runway at London Airport that evening at 9.30 p.m., and crashed, killing everybody on board, both crew and passengers. Five of my friends were on the plane, but I wasn't. When I heard about it on the news the next morning, it gave me a very nasty feeling in my stomach, and still does.

Bill Stirling was a fine man and an outstanding soldier. He was a colonel, and his brother David a major, in the Scots Guards during the Second World War. When serving in North Africa, they decided that the best thing to defeat Rommel was to create a commando-style group of soldiers who would go behind the German lines and blow up their planes, armament and equipment. Their ideas went all the way to the top. From the start Churchill approved the initiative, thinking it an excellent concept, and the War Office gave it the go-ahead. This was the start of what was to become the Special Air Service, whose first operation was to drop men from light planes, to avoid radar, in France and Yugoslavia and other locations.

In peacetime, David Stirling remained a soldier at heart. He loathed Communism, saw it as a threat to Britain, and drew up plans to protect the nation by forming what was to all intents a private army. As it happened, nothing came of the idea. Both brothers, the most loyal of patriots, are now dead.

It was on another evening at John Aspinall's house just off Belgrave Square that my turn came to make a punishing loss at the tables. It was nothing to Bill Stirling's £100,000—but in the mid 1960s it was still a considerable amount of money. Earlier in the evening, before play began in earnest, I wanted to go and spend a penny.

John's wife Jane—a very lovely girl, who was known as the Spirit of Park Lane—told me to go up and use their bathroom upstairs. I walked into the bedroom and there was a large tiger cub on the bed. We looked at each other—and I went to the bathroom pretty quickly and shot the bolt.

Jane, who really was a beautiful creature, had come downstairs in a stunning dress, all glittering with diamonds—having just emerged from a zoo, for the bedroom was thick with tiger turds. There was always a story going the rounds that Aspinall liked having the tiger around because it scratched his back while he was screwing his wife!

Later I was having a very bad night at the tables. But by about 3 a.m. I reckoned I had just about turned the hump and was on my way to a slow and painful recovery. Then at about 4 o'clock, several people decided to go home, by which time there were only four of us left at the table, and not enough to go on with the game. I was swearing under my breath, because my losses, with no chance of pulling back on them, were £10,000.

Over the previous three weeks I'd won some £9,000, but it had all gone, God knows on what. I couldn't pay Aspinall right away, but it was paid eventually, for I regard gambling debts as debts of honour.

It was a bad time altogether. I couldn't avoid the realisation that my drink problem was getting progressively worse; and that my finances were ruinous through my gambling.

Masking my feelings, I said goodnight and asked a footman to call me a taxi. It arrived, but one of the other players pinched it. What the hell, it was a beautiful morning and I decided to walk, and ambled round Belgrave Square, heading for home in South Audley Street.

Then a grotty old Ford Zephyr pulled up beside me and an awful old bag leaned out of the window.

'Want to come home with me, ducks?'

'No, thank you. I haven't got a penny on me. But I'll come home with you if you'll make me a cup of coffee.'

I got into the car, which stank of boiled sweets, and dozed. The next thing I knew was that a lot of men with baskets on their heads were strolling past the Zephyr. We were in Covent Garden. We got out, and went into the woman's seedy apartment nearby, where we were greeted by a damn great unfriendly dog. She made me a cup of coffee, as promised, and pressed into my hands some dog-eared dirty postcards, in the hope of raising my libido. I pushed them away.

'I'm leaving now. I'm not afraid of your dog, and furthermore I know the number of your car. If you don't carry out your part of the bargain, I'll call the police.'

Why I got myself involved in all this, I'll never know. But she gave way, led me back to the car and drove towards Mayfair.

We were in Piccadilly, just outside Simpson's, when her car ran out of petrol. It was now 7.30 a.m. I got out and helped her push the vehicle on to the left-hand side of the street. Then, despite her loud complaints at my leaving her to cope, I walked away, heading for South Audley Street. I was at exactly the same distance from there as I had been three hours earlier.

Still, there were much more agreeable compensations to be found in London. Like the one in the shape of Countess Cowley, the one and only Janet. She was the daughter of an Indian doctor who lived in North Wales and had married a Welsh girl. The resultant progeny was dynamite, was nuclear! Slim, black hair, dark eyed, a beautiful Eurasian colour, wicked sense of humour—and passionate about deep sea fishing. Later I persuaded her to come out to Jamaica and stay with me, that is, live with me, which she did for a time, though she was still married to Earl Cowley.

She and her husband Dennis owned a house in Market Mews, just off Shepherd's Market, where I spent a lot of time with her. One morning Janet went out early, which was unusual for her. Soon afterwards the front door bell rang. I stuck my head out of the window upstairs and saw a man in a bowler hat outside the door. I went down and opened the door and the bowler hat enquired: 'Lord Kimberley?'

'No', I barked. 'I am not Lord Kimberley. I'm Lord Cowley. Just where is that bloody Kimberley'. He took off his hat and stammered: 'Er, er, I'm sorry, m'Lord', and walked away. I discovered later, it was about a Diners Club bill for £68. I quite enjoyed it.

I didn't take Janet off Dennis. He'd already buggered off with a chorus girl from Churchill's nightclub, with whom he was living and had a baby. So when he came round to Market Mews one evening and told me he was going to cite me in his divorce case against Janet, I told him that he must be out of his mind. But he did serve the papers against me, nonetheless, and they were duly divorced, the press taking real pleasure in this 'Earl cites Earl' story.

He died soon afterwards—on the job with a prostitute in the Bayswater Road. He had a heart attack. Serve him right.

Janet and I had many happy days and months together, though I'm glad I didn't marry her. It was like living with an unexploded bomb—but life was never dull. She had these wicked and terribly humorous eyes, and a sense of humour to go with them. Most of all, Janet had a gift for making people laugh, whether she knew them or not. I was devoted to her, and she to me, but I think to have married her would have been another failure in my life.

In the end we just drifted apart. The affair had run its course, though it had been a long one for me. The next thing I knew, she had married Piers Dixon, Tory MP for Truro. The story is told that a woman friend of Janet's was talking to her about an acquaintance.

'I'm surprised you don't know him', she said. 'He's a peer, Lord so-and-so.'

'Don't talk to me about peers', retorted Janet. 'I've had more peers than you've had hot dinners.'

Whether she was referring to 'Piers' or 'Peers', Janet, Countess Cowley would know exactly what she was talking about.

If this most agreeable of affairs had run its course, so had my time as a public relations man. Booze and gambling had taken their toll, PR profits were slim and it was time for a change of life. I sold up John Kimberley Associates, rather badly, to Bertie Joel, who'd made his fortune out of reference books, topped by Kemp's Directories. Within weeks, I'd packed my bags and was on my way to Jamaica.

TEN

JAMAICA AND JANEY

Jamaica was far from new to me. I'd taken holidays there several times, including one with Maggie, my fourth countess—which as it happens ties in neatly with a story about that stunning jazz singer, Peggy Lee. When my PR firm was flying high, I received a telegram from Hollywood asking me to look after Peggy during a month-long cabaret season she was to do in London. Then a call came through from her agent, Jim Mahony, who also represented Frank Sinatra.

'What rate will I be paid?' I asked.

After a bit of horse-trading, we agreed on a small fee with a large expense account.

Peggy arrived and, being a lady who liked the best, insisted on staying at the Dorchester—and in the very expensive Oliver Messel Suite. Her opening night was in a ghastly nightclub in Piccadilly (her choice, not mine!) owned by a man named Bill Ofner, another Pole and conman from the same pack of partridges as John Mills, whom we met in the last chapter. Despite the venue, I assembled a top-line audience for the event.

The season went well, so Peggy extended her London stay considerably, while still ensconced at the Dorchester in one of the highest-priced suites in town. I ended up having to pay her bill of $6,000, a fair sum in the early Sixties! It was to take a very long time before the money could be prised out of her agent in Los Angeles.

On our return from our Jamaica holiday, Maggie and I came via Los Angeles, where we stayed for a few days at the Beverley Hills Hotel. It just happened that Jim Mahony's office was only a couple of blocks away. I rang him.

'I am two blocks from you. You owe me a total of $10,000, and I want it.'

'Gee, I'm so sorry, Peggy's had trouble with her accountant and the tax people.'

'I'm coming round to your office now, and I expect the money to be waiting for me.'

'No, don't do that. I'll bring it round to your hotel right away.'

Which he did. Strange, but if you're on their doorstep, the Americans will pay up promptly. If they owe money in Europe, they think it's out of sight and out of mind, and ignore it. They're quite amoral about it. Still, that LA stop-over did the trick—and it paid for our Jamaica trip.

Early in the year in which I went to live in Jamaica, 1965, I was staying in London with Sir Bruce Tuck Bt, a characterful friend whose family escutcheon was mildly stained when he was cashiered from the Scots Guards for black market dealing in Berlin at the end of the war. He already lived and worked on the island, selling real estate through a company called Graham Associates, which was originally started by Lord Ronald Graham, younger brother of the Duke of Montrose.

I'd been trying to find a girl who would go out to Jamaica with me, and Bruce introduced me to Gillian Raw. Two or three days before Bruce and I were to leave London, Gillian came to dinner with us. At the end of the evening I asked:

'Would you like to come out to the West Indies with me?'

Without hesitation she said, 'Yes'.

When we arrived in Jamaica, I found that Bruce's business partner, Nigel Pemberton, had found a flat for me to live in, which was comparatively cheap, but rather small. So Bruce and his girlfriend and Gillie and I decided we'd rent a house together, and there we lived for about six months.

Immediately below us, down the hill, was a house which was owned and lived in by a Polish 'royal' named Prince Korybut, who was also a fashionable architect on the island. Most of the houses in our locality had been designed by him. He had a knack—in which his title helped, no doubt—of sliding smoothly into all the highest social niches and of getting a toe into everything. Thus he was known as the Worm!

He had a girlfriend called Joan Morse, who had her own house a couple of miles away. She had a big dinner party one evening, and afterwards we all felt very peculiar.

'Hope you all enjoyed your soup', she said later.

'Yes, very much.'

'Good, I put LSD in it.'

Most of us had hallucinations, and it wasn't very funny. Particularly so for me, because by now my drinking problem was getting progressively worse. It was encouraged by the job I was doing, selling real estate to Americans and renting houses to them. Lovely houses they were too, fully staffed and pretty expensive, and bringing in for me a healthy 10 per cent commission.

I had to drink! Where was I going to find the right clients? In the leading hotels, of course, which I frequented constantly, getting to know barmen and staff so I knew who was staying. I got quite good at sorting the wheat from the chaff and getting rid of the time-wasters.

But hitting the bottle so hard meant I was in a daze each morning. My answer was to dive into a swimming pool to clear my head for the day's work—and drinking—ahead.

After six months, Gillie returned to England. At the time it suited me fine, because I confess I was getting bored with her. But as we shall see, she was to come back into my life in a big way.

Soon afterwards I was despatched to the islands of Grenada and Trinidad to look at some property. Grenada was the more beautiful of the two, with property which was out of this world, the best of it being on a peninsula, but all long since swept aside to make way for the island's international airport, built for it by the old Soviet Union.

Where the isthmus joined the property to the island was only 20 yards wide. But one side was the Atlantic and on the other side, the Caribbean. On the Atlantic side was black volcanic sand. On the other side, the sand was silver. The property I was there to look at had horses and sheep, all carefully looked after. Paradise.

From Grenada I flew on to Port of Spain, Trinidad, where I had a reservation at the Hilton—in the name of Lord and Lady Kimberley. I checked in and made sure I had the double room and double bed I'd asked for, in anticipation of finding a lady friend to share it with that night. At five o'clock in the morning I turned up with a Trinidadian limbo dancer!

'You can't come in here', said the concierge.

'Look at your register', I said.

He did, looked up and replied:

'Beg your pardon, m'Lord.'

There wasn't much of the night to go, but they were interesting hours. Pleasure in limbo, you might say.

Back in Jamaica, I had a house on my books which I particularly wanted to sell. Handsome place, traditional Jamaican with a shingle roof, and a swimming pool in the grounds. I had a potential buyer who was staying at Round Hill, the hotel which was the 'in' place to stay in those days.

When I turned up at the hotel to pick up my client, he wasn't there. But someone else asked to look at the property. It was John Clark, chairman of Plessey, the international electronics company. He looked at the place, liked it and bought it, for a cool £100,000, a lot of money in the late Sixties, and providing me with a very nice commission.

Round Hill, three miles west of Montego Bay, was a cottage development, each guest having his own little house. I remember meeting an American who was staying there whom I recall because of his name—Oscar Seabass. He had his own little house called Martini Manor. Resident owner of Round Hill was a very rich man named John Pringle, Scottish in origin, and a very sociable and thoroughly nice individual, but not a man to be taken on lightly.

One evening I dined there with an old friend, Arthur 'Butch' Bullen, a rough diamond Cockney, known for his fiery temper, who had made himself a fortune. We arrived with our respective partners, having travelled up to Round Hill in my funny little hire car, a baby Ford, which was all one needed there.

Dinner was a black tie job, out of doors, with John Pringle hosting a party of a dozen leading socialites from America and London. Among them, as I recall, was Fred Astaire's sister Adèle, who had once been married to a cousin of the Duke of Devonshire.

As we arrived, I'd passed my car keys to one of the hotel staff and asked him to park the vehicle for me. Dinner ended, I called a waiter and requested that the car be brought round for us. He came back to say that the outside staff couldn't get it to start. Before I could stop him, Butch was on his feet and stalking towards John Pringle.

'Are you the manager?'

'No. I own the hotel.'

'Then one of your staff has damaged my friend's car. Get it mended', demanded a now angry Butch.

Pringle, still sitting at table among his guests, looked up at him and said warningly:

'If you don't stop yelling, I'll have you thrown out of my hotel.'

To which came the sparky response:

'If you don't do as I say, I'll buy your bloody hotel.'

Another car was produced, and we left. Next day, I persuaded Butch to write a letter of apology to John Pringle. But the story reverberated around the island for months.

Another extremely well-heeled individual whom I met while trying to flog a house to him was the delightful president of the American Eastern Airlines Company, though his name, alas, has disappeared from my memory. But what I do remember is his invitation to fly down with him to Trinidad for the weekend.

He would fly me there himself, he explained, piloting his personal Lear jet. He was 78! I was in my forties and had only ever flown an Auster. What would I do if he had a heart attack at 40,000 feet? I decided not to go, and politely declined the invitation.

Then came a diversion from the daily round which would be forever memorable—my first and last film appearance. The film in question was called *Skulduggery*. It was made by Universal, shot just outside Montego Bay and had a $20,000,000 budget.

I got back from a weekend in Palm Beach to be greeted by Victor, my houseman.

'Lord, they want you in a movie!', he announced in his irresistible Jamaican accent.

'Victor, don't talk balls.'

'Yes Lord, you must ring up Mr So and So at the Royal Caribbean Hotel.'

So I did, and it was true. The next morning I went round to the hotel and saw the gentleman in question, whose name now eludes me, and he really was offering me a part—albeit a small one. The director of the movie was Gordon Douglas, who directed all Frank Sinatra's pictures.

Skulduggery was without doubt one of the worst movies ever made. On the list of credits it had Burt Reynolds, Chips Rafferty, Wilfrid Hyde White, ·Edward Fox, a stage actor from New York called Roger Carmel—and John Kimberley.

I got hold of the script and found that I played the part of an Englishman who was the public relations man to the Government of the Northern Territory of Australia—the colonial representative so to speak, with the illustrious name of Epstein. This was about the time of the Beatles, so I thought it was brilliant.

My first words on the Technicolour screen were 'Good morning', as Reynolds and Carmel arrived in Northern Territory.

I said to Gordon Douglas the night before: 'Gordon, how do you want me to say "good morning"?'

After all, you can say it in a hundred different ways. And I, John Kimberley, was thinking of getting an Oscar for Best Supporting

Actor.

Douglas's reply was devastatingly to the point:

'Say it any goddam fucking way you like.'

Discouraged, I went to wardrobe to find a suit. They hadn't got anything that fitted me so I wore my own lightweight suits—which they paid for. The wardrobe master and I introduced ourselves.

'Good to meet you, Johnny. What size suit do you wear?'

'I'm sorry, but I don't know.'

'But you must have a suit size.'

'No, in London I have my clothes made for me.'

'Oh! Gee, I wish I could have a custom-built suit.'

This was all deadly serious. I had to struggle not to laugh. But I still had to wear my own clothes.

We had two lots of night shooting which was very cold, believe it or not, because the location was up a mountain and at 2,000 feet even in Jamaica it gets bloody chilly. After the first night, I took up a few bottles of Scotch and got everybody pissed, technicians, actors, everybody. But we were warmer. And we didn't crash the helicopter—an important prop—or kill anybody either, which was probably a miracle.

I talked to the film executives and asked them how much they were going to pay me for my part.

'Fifty dollars', came the reply.

'No you won't', says I. 'You'll give me a contract like any other actor'.

After all, I knew a thing or two about show business from my public relations days. So I got a reasonable contract and they had to go on paying me as long as it took to make the film.

Anyway, at the beginning of the film I appeared on a jetty to welcome these two foreigners (Reynolds and Carmel) to Australia. They had been to New Guinea and found the 'Missing Link', intelligent little people who were played by funny little Japanese actors and actresses, who were heavily made up and covered in hair. The plot included a helicopter flight—and no sooner were these clever mini human beings aboard than they knew how to fly it. We had hysterics.

I didn't win Best Supporting Actor. Nor did I ever appear on screen again. Later, I got an agent when I got back to England, but unless you'd been to RADA you couldn't get a ticket and you couldn't get a ticket until you'd performed. Catch 22 strikes again.

The only thing I did learn on the *Skulduggery* set was an outrage-
ous doggerel verse which I got from Burt Reynolds's stand-in:

> Once upon a time in China
> Lived two Chinamen
> Called Ikum and Nokum.
> Nokum was married to a beautiful
> Chinese girl called Nokum Too,
> While Ikum was single.
>
> One day Ikum went over the mountains
> To visit his friend Nokum
> But Nokum wasn't at home.
> So Nokum Too, with Chinese hospitality,
> Invited Ikum to stay the night.
> That night Nokum Too came
> And Ikum was so happy that he came to.
>
> Later on Nokum found out that
> He was going to become a father
> And he wondered how come.
> So when the baby was born,
> He called it How Kum U Kum.
>
> Now Nokum Too and Ikum knew how
> How Kum U Kum came,
> But to this day,
> Nokum doesn't know how,
> How Kum U Kum came.

I wrote it down in pencil on the back of the script because I knew
I would never remember it. But it took even longer to learn.

A forever memorable experience, is how I described the *Skulddug-
gery* episode. But it pales into insignificance, as far as my existence
is concerned, beside the day when I walked into a cocktail party at
the Bay Rock Hotel on Montego Bay. Across the room I saw a very
tall, very striking girl, very bronzed and with pale blue eyes. I was
transfixed.

I hadn't seen her around before, which surprised me, as I had an
attentive eye for pretty girls in the locality. I walked up to her and

asked:

'How did you get past my intelligence agency without my spotting you earlier? You've obviously been here for a long time. Look at the colour of you.'

It was love at first sight. Jane Consett, my future sixth countess, had come into my life.

If there were any doubts about the emotional thunderbolt that had hit me they were removed the following Sunday, when I invited Janey to a picnic with friends in an incredibly beautiful place in the jungle, where there are seven waterfalls and you can dive from one rock pool into another. And there are no crocodiles!

'May I bring some food?', she asked.

She would say that, so typical and thoughtful.

'I'll bring some potatoes in their jackets.'

It sounded odd to me, but they went down a treat. So did our mutual attraction. That afternoon, we were both in love. More, I adored and worshipped her. More than 30 years on, I still do.

I asked her to come and stay with me. A week later—a very long week for me—she duly arrived on the local bus from Falmouth (which seemed to be significant, considering my old family interests in Falmouth, Cornwall). The bus was full of singing, laughing Jamaican women.

As the bus pulled away, I noticed that Janey had no luggage except a couple of plastic bags.

'Where's your luggage?', I asked.

'Oh my God, I've left it on the BUS.'

I telephoned the chief of police, an enchanting Jamaican and great friend, Owen Stephenson. A divine man, with a great sense of humour, very good looking and often a dinner guest in my house. Just a great guy. When he answered the telephone I explained the situation and asked:

'Owen, could you get one of your boys to "arrest" Janey's luggage please?'

The errant luggage was delivered to my door that same afternoon.

It was accepted almost at once that Janey and I would live together. It all happened so naturally, and we had a deeply passionate affair. Before, I'd been inviting to Jamaica women I'd met in Europe and America, juggling arrivals and departures so that one wasn't flying in before the other had left. It was a near thing, once or twice. When Janey came into my life, it was the first time that I'd been absolutely faithful to one woman. It was peaceful and tranquil. 'The deep, deep peace of the double bed, as opposed to the hurly-burly of the *chaise-longue*', as wise old Mrs Patrick Campbell put it.

That was in November 1969. But despite the happiness Janey had brought me, I had problems. I was heavily in debt, and though it was to be some time before I admitted it, I was a full-blown alcoholic. Four months later I deserted Janey and flew back to England, alone—though not before I'd shaken off a bank manager intent on keeping me in Jamaica until I'd cleared an overdraft.

It was sorted out for me by a colleague in the real estate business, Michael Lloyd, who became a very good friend through the years that followed. We called him Rillage, because he had crinkly hair, like little waves (from 'rill', a small stream or a rivulet).

I remember that as the plane bringing me back flew over Devon and Cornwall, heading for London, the whole country was under snow. It was unforgettable, but it didn't help my depression. Nor the guilt I felt at leaving Janey behind because, daughter of a lieutenant-colonel who'd won the DSO and MC though she was, she was a working girl. A girl who, to put it bluntly, wasn't well off enough to support me in the manner to which I was accustomed. At least, that's how I looked at it then. But it was my deranged alcoholic brain that was talking.

Thus I arrived at Heathrow, broke by my standards, no roof over my head, alcoholic and deep in depression. The situation did at least force me to make a start at sorting out the family holdings in Falmouth, which kept me afloat then and still do, although they are getting less and less.

But my first action, driven by desperation, I suppose, was to ring Gillie Raw, who was living in quite a nice basement flat in Rutland Gate in Knightsbridge. When I explained my predicament she said:

'Well, you'd better come here.'

It worked quite well. Her stepmother Barbara and her father, Colonel Norman Ireland-Smith, often invited us down to their home near Sherborne, in Somerset, a lovely old house which made it appear that they had quite a lot of money. In fact, they hadn't.

Still, they were pleasant times. I went shooting one day with Norman at a place called Cricket St Thomas. The first thing I saw was a partridge coming over the hedge—on a giraffe's head. A slightly unusual sight in the depths of the English countryside. I soon discovered that there was a zoo there. Later Cricket St Thomas was to be the village where the television series, *To the Manor Born*, was filmed.

I'd arrived back in London on 1 March 1970. In no time I'd proposed to Gillie. Even now I've no idea what possessed me. The only answer is my deep need for security, which has always held me in its grip. By July we were, fatefully, man and wife. We were married in the country somewhere on the edge of Somerset and Dorset, followed by a reception at the Ireland-Smiths' home.

I ask myself again: Why did I propose? A sense of survival, I suppose. And the fact that we'd had quite an affair five years earlier in Jamaica. But I didn't love her.

I still didn't have anywhere of my own to live. I went down to Falmouth to see my agent, and we found a minute dairy farm on a creek off the Helford River, near a sweet little village called Constantine. Through the astuteness of my trustees, there was still a little money left in the financial wreckage, enough to buy the farm.

Nonsuch (for so I called it, after a hill in Norfolk) came with a herd of cows, plus a very good cowman. It was all very attractive—a land of milk and honey where you'd probably get kicked by a cow and stung by a bee (as the saying goes). The river was tidal and came up the creek, bringing with it shoals of mullet.

There was, however, 200 yards from the farmhouse, a ghastly modern house, lived in by the fellow from whom we bought the farm. There was a shared drive between the properties, which is never a good idea.

All the fields had water laid on for the cattle, but the pipes were put in too shallow, so they were constantly breaking and leaking and millions of gallons of water, for all of which I was paying by meter, were disappearing. It was also very difficult to find out where all the pipes were, as there was no map.

Still, it was a most beautiful place and I loved it. I made a garden in twelve months, helped by the wonderful climate in Cornwall, redecorated the house and made it really charming.

To begin with, Gillie and I lived in a caravan until the house had been made habitable. I remember hearing on the wireless in the caravan that the Conservatives had been elected, with Ted Heath at their head, which dates it pretty firmly as 1970.

By the time Gillie and I had been together two years, there wasn't any pleasure in it any more. There wasn't any fun. There had been a time when we did things together, and enjoyed each other's company.

51 Gillie, Johnny's fifth wife.

When we were in Jamaica, I used to take her out deep sea fishing in Montego Bay. In Cornwall, we went out shark fishing, which was a great hobby of mine and she thoroughly enjoyed it too.

I founded a shark fishing club in Falmouth, and made its headquarters a pub called the Norway Inn, run by Billy Herbert, another shark enthusiast. Sooner than I realised, both pub and landlord were to play a vital role in my story.

As tensions between Gillian and myself worsened, a point came where I was thinking:

'What am I doing living in a house with a woman I don't like and who doesn't like me?'

If I looked at it soberly—if that was possible at the time—the marriage had been a disaster from the start. Gillie was fine as a girl friend, but not as a wife. She was drinking too, and we had the most frightful fights. It was the perfect scenario for my old drink problem to reassert itself, and it did. I'd had bad times before, but in the few months ahead I was to go through hell and back because of alcohol. I was drinking like fury—a bottle of spirits a day and more besides.

I got terribly depressed and everything I touched turned to dust. Some of the time I was quite out of my mind. I mean, would a normal person try to drive his car up the steps of the Norfolk Hotel at Brighton?

I'd tried to beat it. At one point I used a system of going off the booze for a month, then on it for three months. But the month got shorter and the three months longer.

One Sunday morning I was lying in my bath at the farmhouse. I looked out of the window and the scene was beautiful, as beautiful as the countryside can be. But darker thoughts were in my head. For the first time, suddenly, I made the awful admission to myself that I was an alcoholic. I felt trapped, helpless, like a rat up a drainpipe with a brick in the end. I thought to myself:

'I don't see any way out of this. Except to go out on the farm with one of my guns and blow my head off.'

The thought was real and serious. Then I remembered at that moment that someone had told me that Billy Herbert at the Norway Inn was a reformed alcoholic who had joined Alcoholics Anonymous.

We had guests staying that weekend. A friend of Gillian's, Anthony Montague Browne, who had been Winston Churchill's private secretary, came down with his wife Shelagh. It was her second marriage. Her first husband was Lance Callingham, a famous racing driver who was caught up in a terrible accident at Le Mans which sent a car roaring into the crowd, killing a large number of people.

That evening I drove them and their dog to Truro station to get the night train back to London. I came back, very pissed, and knowing that I had to do something if I didn't want to be destroyed. On impulse I drove to the Norway Inn and asked for a double brandy. I sat staring at it and said:

'Billy, I think I have a problem. I don't think I can beat the Demon Alcohol. I have been trying for long enough.'

We talked about AA and Billy promised to take me to a meeting a couple of nights later in St Austell. The evening came and a friend of his picked me up and took me to the home of the head of the local AA group. There were several men present, and one woman, about eight of us in all. We introduced ourselves just by our Christian names.

Each person round the circle told a little vignette of his life. After I'd heard all of them I reckoned I could pick a little piece from each one and apply it to myself.

At the end of the meeting I was given a cup of tea and a biscuit, instead of my usual large vodka and tonic, and I thought to myself:

'Jesus Christ, if I'd been told about this 24 hours ago, I'd have roared with laughter.'

Then we all stood up and said goodnight. That was it. No chit-chat. As I was walking out, Billy stopped me:

'The next meeting is next Tuesday and you will come to it.'

It wasn't an invitation. It was an order, and I obeyed it. From that night on I was on the wagon, and by the time I left Cornwall I had started three more Alcoholics Anonymous branches and helped a lot of people. Later on I would take that commitment still further—to the red leather benches of the House of Lords.

If this was a vital new beginning, there was yet another end and beginning waiting at the farm—the misery of my marriage with Gillian and how to make the inevitable break. I had lived with her drunk, and now I was living with her sober—and living with her sober was even worse.

Alcoholics Anonymous has a marvellous prayer, and this, if ever, was a time to put it into practice: 'God grant me the serenity to accept the things I cannot change; the courage to change the things I can; and the wisdom to know the difference.'

What I could and had to do was get rid of Gillian from the farm—but I had a hell of a job to do it. I paid for her to move her furniture and she went, I don't know where. When she'd gone I breathed a huge sigh of relief. With it, of course, came another major blow to my finances—though as the wives went on, the pay-offs became less and less, because there was less and less available to pay out. The cake is only so big.

I had a good lawyer named David Leverton, one of the best divorce lawyers in England. I'd known him for years, but for some reason I'd never used him before. God, how I wish I had. I told him, without beating around the bush, that I had no money.

'But somehow, get me a divorce from this woman.'

And somehow he did, and I paid £10,000 to be rid of her. Within a month she had married again. For me, things were to move more slowly, for I knew then, as I'd known in my heart of hearts from the day I flew out of Jamaica three years earlier, that I had to find Janey again and get her back.

Early on my search for her drew a blank, and I was frantic. She'd left Jamaica and gone to live with a girl friend in Antigua. The only addresses I had were her mother's house in Coln St Denis, in Gloucestershire, and a flat in London where one of her sisters lived. I wrote to Janey through both of them. Then I managed to discover that she was working her way home across the Atlantic as cook on a small sailing ship. She loved sailing and the merry adventures it brought, as I was to discover.

A very old friend of hers, who quickly became a great friend of mine, is Jeremy Churcher, who has led a life as colourful as James Bond's and twice as unlikely, is a natural storyteller, and who at one time was skipper of his own ocean-going yacht. He tells with brio a tale involving Janey some time before I met her. It's his story, so I'll let him tell it:

> I'd been skippering my yacht in the Med when I got a telephone call from Janey's sister Sophie, asking if there was a place on board, as cook or something similar, for Janey to cross with us to the West Indies. No problem, I said.
>
> I gave the approximate dates we would be leaving certain places—the South of France, Majorca, Alicante, Gibraltar. So at each of these bloody places we delayed, but no Janey. But Sophie had been insistent—'We've heard she's left … She's on her way … Do just hang on a bit'. So we did.
>
> But the problem was that, to cross the Atlantic, the best sailing month was December and we didn't want to miss the wind. Anyway, the news came through eventually that Janey had got herself on to a ferry boat heading for the Canary Islands.

There we sat, ten of us in all, awaiting the elusive Janey. We were at anchor off the port, because it cost less than lying by the dock. But the night before our departure ('Whether Janey arrives or not', we'd said) we had to come alongside to take on water.

That evening, when everything had been loaded and checked, I grabbed the chance to take my Irish setter for a walk ashore. He appreciated it too, sniffing and lifting his leg at every-thing—after all, this was his last chance ashore for many weeks. It was about 5.30 to 6 p.m., and we were passing the local bank. From inside I heard a raised English voice complaining rather crossly: 'But bloody hell, man, it's a Coutts cheque. Everybody takes a Coutts cheque'.

My dog, intrigued, trotted into the bank to investigate. A moment later, out came Janey, rather annoyed, and still clutching her cheque. I called out to her and you could see the relief when she saw me. 'Thank God you've come in time. I'm trying to cash some money to pay for my ferry trip'.

But how did you come, for three days from Barcelona on a Spanish ferry to the Canary Islands, without paying for the trip?

The answer was pure Janey: 'Ah well, I met this German called Helmut. He's a physical training instructor, a real Kraut who wears a tracksuit and is always bouncing around. I promised him I would pay him back when we got to the Canaries. He's been chasing me round the decks and now he's determined to have his pound of flesh unless I pay him. But these bloody Spaniards won't cash my cheque'.

We squared Helmut for her—but he had a very sorry look on his face when we said goodbye, and set sail for the Caribbean.

But to return to that nail-biting time when Janey was making the east–west Atlantic crossing, and I was waiting in Cornwall, all anxiety and impatience for news. I wrote again care of her mother's and sister's addresses: 'Please will you ring me when you get back to England?'

The wait seemed interminable, for I was not to know that there had been mutinous troubles aboard the boat, and that Janey had been dumped ashore in Portugal. From there, self-confident as ever, she'd cheerfully hitch-hiked to the Channel. But that, and more, is her story, which she tells as postscript to this book—with not a single word censored by me!

Then came the call I'd prayed for. Janey rang me from Cheltenham, I sent her rail tickets to Truro, and we were reunited. That was nearly 30 years ago, and we've never been apart since. I'd always believed it could happen. And with Janey the dream came true.

ELEVEN

THE HOUSE OF LORDS

When I met Janey at Truro station, I took her back to my little farm, and there we lived happily for a couple of years. They were important years for me in other ways too. Not only was I firmly on the wagon. I was fit and well again, and eager to do something useful with my changed life.

With Janey's encouragement, I began attending the House of Lords, as an hereditary peer. I'd taken my seat in 1945, but I was living in Norfolk then and didn't really want to go to London every week. Now I was determined to make up for the lost years. I was very anti-Communist, and felt it was time I did something about politics.

Through that decision, I later became chairman of the National Council on Alcoholism, as I'll be relating in due course. It also prompted our move out of Cornwall.

The problem was that, if I was to take membership of the Lords seriously, it was completely impractical to keep going up to London from way down in the toe of England. Even if I flew, there was an hour's drive to Newquay, and then the long haul into Westminster at the other end. So the logical thing was to live in or near London.

So the farm of which I was so fond was sold. But at least its pretty situation ensured that it went for a very good price. We came first to Gloucestershire, where we moved into Janey's mother's house, Botany House, near Fossebridge. Meantime, our search went on for a suitable property we might buy.

We'd looked at about 50 houses over a period of seven or eight months when I saw in *Country Life* a picture of Hailstone House, in Wiltshire, about 14 miles away from Fossebridge, and liked it at once. I walked in through the main door and saw the view opposite, across fields and trees, and with the infant River Thames at the bottom of the garden. I just fell for it.

A few years later, when we were securely settled in, an *Evening Standard* feature writer came to interview me, and for me delightfully caught the image both of the setting and the house:

The Earl lives in Wiltshire in an elegant house, below which the land falls away in terraces to the Thames. There were watercolours and magazines and baskets of logs, a bust of Lord Kimberley with his Guards cap on it; a picture of the young Lord K. on a polo pony; all the comfort and clutter beloved of the English upper classes.

I don't think it's changed much since then, even to my old Guards cap perched rakishly on the bust. But when I first fell for the house, I was the only one who did. Neither Janey, her mother, nor my son Henry liked it, and were all opposed to my buying it. But I refused to be put off. Yet they all came round in time, and Janey came to love the place as much as I do. Now everyone says how clever I was to buy it, but in fact it was a fluke

That was in October 1975. It was not until 20 August 1982 that we married. We plighted our troth, I remember, at a renowned fish restaurant in Chelsea called La Poissonière. There was a large bowl of crudités on the table. Janey took a stick of celery from it, and was about to cut it when her knife slipped, and gashed one of her hands. There was blood all over the table and its snowy white cloth.

It could have been at that same restaurant—it was certainly in Chelsea—that Janey and I were dining a few years later, and I had my last sight of Gillian. There she was, looking very good. She came over and spoke to us in that deep, husky voice of hers, and very affably introduced herself to Janey.

'I am your predecessor.'

Returning to that 'betrothal night' in 1975, all that blood around might have seemed a bad omen. But I knew that this time, at last, after six times the trying, that I had got it right. Despite all the disasters, I still remained an optimist underneath. I believe that if you strive for perfection, eventually you'll find it.

I've always liked being married, perhaps because it gives me a feeling of security. I hated being alone. Each time I thought: This is going to be it! And at last it was, and darling Janey is the proof.

On the night of our wedding, we had dinner at the home of the Henriques family between Cirencester and Cheltenham—Robert Henriques was a well known author who wrote novels about Gloucestershire farms, shooting and countryside. There were about ten of us there that evening. I was introduced as Johnny Kimberley and

Janey as Janey Consett—until I put it right:

'We were married today. She is now Janey Kimberley.'

Champagne, as I recall, was served immediately, and congratulations showered upon us.

It was now a new life opening up to me. Taking my seat in the Lords became a routine part of my life, two or three days a week and more, and I soon became recognised as an established figure in the House and its affairs.

The long haul from Cornwall to SW1 had been a real inconvenience. Now even commuting from Wiltshire seemed hard work, on such a regular basis. So I sold off a chunk of the Hailstone House property to finance a flat in London, within walking distance of the Lords.

While still in Cornwall I'd sorted out my political affiliation. Within the county there were a lot of Liberals, but there was also the influence of my Wodehouse family tradition of Liberal politics. My great-grandfather was a member of the party. My father fought and won Mid Norfolk as a Liberal—though, as will be recalled from an earlier chapter, not exactly for political reasons!

In any event, I couldn't stand Harold Wilson, and didn't much care for Edward Heath either. My dislike of Wilson was confirmed when he observed to me one day:

'You were a fool to join the Army when war broke out. I joined the civil service.'

But I did like Lord (Frank) Byers, who had fought in the war and was leading the Liberals in the Lords. So I went in under Frank's tuition and accepted the party's whip. At that time there were not many Liberals in the Lords, so one could be a reasonable fish in a small pool.

After a few weeks there was a debate on agriculture. Byers suggested I should take up the subject as my maiden speech. Of course I'd run the Kimberley estate years before, but I confessed I didn't know much about agriculture in the 1970s. So I took the line of agriculture being used as a political football. At the turn of the millennium, nothing has changed.

Naturally I was nervous. But I made it—I felt almost that I had swum the Channel!

After that I never stopped talking. There were so few Liberals in the Lords then that someone had to talk when debates came up, and it was often me.

52 Johnny, Janey (his sixth wife) and Alan Saville at a wedding.

Mind you, I didn't turn my nose up at the chance to learn how to do the job properly. A political friend of mine told me about his speech trainer, and advised that I use his services too. I took the advice and it was well worth the trouble. So was a television and wireless course I did in North London. One of the teachers was the splendid Sue Lawley, of *Desert Island Discs*, who was very good indeed. I suppose it was all basic common sense really, but it served to underline everything and to make you think. And thinking on your feet in the Lords is a useful skill.

In time I became the Liberal party's spokesman on aerospace and defence—two subjects of real interest to me, then and now—and on voluntary community services. The latter was a link with my work on alcoholism.

I was very keen on Concorde, which came into service in 1976,

and is still as eye-catching and beautiful as it ever was—even after
the horrific crash on the outskirts of Paris in July 2000, which sent a
shock-wave around the world. For Concorde was universally seen not
only as a brilliant technological achievement, but as perhaps the safest
aircraft in the skies. I felt an almost personal sense of anguish when
the news of the disaster broke, for I had been closely involved with
Concorde's story from the very start. I can't remember how many
supportive speeches I made on the subject in the Lords, and the
trouble I caused for various ministers. It shouldn't be forgotten that
there were those who were vehemently opposed to it from an early
stage, particularly on the grounds of cost. Fortunately the Anglo-
French contract had a cast-iron clause forbidding withdrawal from the
project at any point.

I spoke angrily about it when Pompidou flew to the Bahamas for
a world summit, in a French Concorde; but Callaghan, then Prime
Minister, chose to fly British Airways rather than in the English
Concorde, flight-worthy as it was, but not yet in service.

During the testing period, I flew with Brian Trubshaw, then chief
test pilot for British Aerospace. Brian, who died shortly before this
book was published, was a happy-go-lucky man who really enjoyed
life. He couldn't have been anything else but a pilot. When he flew,
he was part of the aeroplane. When he was testing a plane, he was
absolutely 100 per cent dedicated to it. He was great fun to be with,
always full of jokes. I don't know how many different kinds of
aircraft he flew in his life, but the number must have been enormous.

Later I flew to Washington and back in Concorde, and had the
excitement of occupying the jump seat in the cockpit when we took
off from London, landed at Washington, and put down at Heathrow
on our return.

About a decade later, in late 1990 I think it was, I was involved
in a very public exchange of words about Concorde with Saatchi &
Saatchi, that plushiest and wealthiest of PR outfits. The row was
about the £135,000 model of the airliner placed on the main roundabout near Heathrow Terminals 1, 2 and 3, which was publicised as
an inspiration of the Saatchi brothers. This, I said in a spiky letter to
British Airways, was absolute rubbish. In fact this latest so-called
Saatchi brainwave had been suggested to BA by me, some 14 years
earlier, when I had proposed that one of the surplus Concordes should
be sited on this very roundabout. The then government had responded
with a firm 'No' and an inference that I should not be so stupid. BA

were said in 1990 to be paying the Saatchi brothers £7 million for their many services. My advice came free!

Going back to the 1970s, I was still having alcohol problems, despite my commitment to Alcoholics Anonymous. So this was my chosen subject for one of my early speeches in the Lords, and no one could doubt my expert knowledge. I disclosed that I was a member of AA. That I chose to give away my anonymity was my business, I told the House. But I would not give away anyone else's. My view was then, and remains, that if people knew I was a reformed alcoholic—or at least, was well on the way to being so—they might listen to me, and I could offer help.

To admit you are an alcoholic is like taking the weight of the world off your shoulders. Just to be able to admit it! They always say: once an alcoholic, always an alcoholic. I often say: I am a recovered alcoholic. But the response to that is to say there's no such thing. I only drink white wine now (with Janey doing her best to ration me even on that). I don't touch spirits any more, not even a dry Martini. I know all the tricks. I used to keep a bottle behind a vase of flowers, and would slide over to it when I thought nobody was looking. I knew those who hid bottles around the garden. You tell me a new way an alcoholic will try to hide his drinking and I bet you I'll know it.

Subsequently I made other speeches in the Lords on alcoholism, and the reaction of fellow peers was very favourable. This led to my appointment as chairman of the National Council on Alcoholism, which proved to be a far from comfortable ride. It was unpaid but I was happy to do it because I knew so much about the problem.

The job took me to Washington to an AA gathering called Operation Understanding, which was full of famous actors and the like, all ready to be recognised as reformed boozers. There I met Dick van Dyke and Buzz Aldrin, the second man on the Moon. I spent 48 hours with him and we never once talked about the moon voyage. He was absolutely charming, and Janey and I still exchange Christmas cards with him and his wife Lois. He's about the same age as me, but looks much younger and is definitely fitter.

It's an odd fact that a lot of astronauts, on returning to Earth, took to the bottle. I remember seeing a film years back, on television, which dealt with just this subject. The poignant conclusion was that, viewed from the moon, our planet looks beautiful, pure, unsullied, serene. But on returning to its surface the astronaut is brought back to the reality of mankind's inhumanity to man and the horrendous things man is doing which are defiling his planet.

Faced with this truth, the voyager can find solace only in drink!

As a result of the Washington conference, I was made a vice-president of the World Council on Alcoholism. It was, I like to think, a step up on my other exalted global role in the Tiddlywinks World Championship. Though the tiddlywinks event did have royal patronage, in the person of the Duke of Edinburgh!

On the political front, my sojourn with the Liberal party was not to be a long one. Two days before the general election on 3 May 1979, I wrote a letter to the *Daily Telegraph*. In it I suggested that, to prevent a left-wing Marxist government getting in under false pretences through a split in the vote, the Liberals would be much better served if they voted Conservative. The letter appeared and David Steel rang me the next day, fired me from my Liberal roles in the Lords—and for good measure booted me out of the party.

For a brief spell I became a cross-bencher. Then my old friend Robert Cecil, Marquess of Salisbury, came to me and persuaded me to go over to the Tories. It was Robert who, 40 years earlier, had persuaded me at 4 o'clock in the morning to become a Grenadier. I'd never for a second regretted that decision. And I've had no reasons either to regret the new decision I then made, even though eighteen years later Tony Blair made me redundant.

By late 1982, things had reached explosion point in the National Council on Alcoholism (now called Alcohol Concern) between the 'reformed alcoholics' side, led by me (I'd been off the booze for a decade by then) and the teetotal brigade. Following a big internal row, the teetotallers left the organisation like lemmings. Derek Rutherford, former NCA director (a staunch left-wing teetotaller, with whom I shared mutual dislike) and Andrew MacNeill, the council's industrial officer, both defected to the UK Temperance Alliance. MacNeill was promptly replaced by another reformed alcoholic.

Then, as *The Times* crisply put it, 'there followed a rather ungracious decision by the Alliance to cease funding the important post of NCA industrial officer.' I retaliated by approaching the Scotch Whisky Association for £25,000 support. They were very friendly about it, but sadly the idea didn't gel. I approached Seagrams too, because I knew the chairman, but that initiative didn't produce the goods either. When *The Times* approached me for a quote, I laid my position on the line: 'I think it's high time the NCA stopped being run by a bunch of Methodist teetotallers, and was run by people like myself who know something about problem drinking.'

I'd also been stirring things up a touch at Alcoholics Anonymous, by arguing that we should be trying to save people before they get into the gutter, and not wait until they were there and then kick them. Prevention, in my view, was better than cure.

Clearly all this didn't go down well with the government. Kenneth Clarke, who was health minister at that time, stepped in and sacked me from my NCA chairmanship. I told him he was a damned fool, and predicted that in my place he would bring in someone who didn't understand alcoholism, and certainly had never been through it. And that is exactly what happened. The replacement was paid, to boot!

There were lighter episodes during the Lords years. Like the February morning when I and three fellow peers brought a touch of early mad March hare spring to Park Lane, to the utter bemusement of onlookers and the delight of Press photographers. Earl Attlee led the frolic, with Lord Redesdale, the Earl of Ilchester and myself. For there we were, all done up in our lordly ermine, leap-frogging over each other in fine style, our robes billowing like exotic wings in the breeze.

But there was method in this noble nonsense. We were on a St John's Ambulance national sponsored leapfrog, which was set to raise £100,000 in—when else—leap year. There was only one spill, when Redesdale didn't quite negotiate Ilchester and the two of them thudded down to a hard landing on this blessed plot.

In different mode, there was the occasion when I had a rather special guest to lunch. I loved the *Steptoe & Son* comedy series on television and, to show my appreciation, I wrote to Harry H. Corbett, telling him how much I enjoyed the show. Would he like to come and join me for lunch in the House of Lords?

He was startled and surprised by the invitation, but he came and we had a jolly time, together with two other peers—which two, I have to confess, I can't recall. Harry was charming. He had an ordinary accent, nothing like the character, and was a very self-effacing man, never trying to hog the conversation. At that time I was very keen to be moving upwards, so I didn't think it would do me any harm with the publicity which arose from it. My fellow peers were much amused by my choice of guest, and everyone wanted to talk to him.

By now I had made myself an authority on aerospace, defence and foreign affairs matters, and was recognised as such. I'd always been interested in aeroplanes and always kept myself up to date. No sooner was I involved in the Lords, than I made a point of making friends with British Aerospace, Vickers and the like.

In the early 1980s I became a parliamentary delegate to the North Atlantic Assembly, which is made up of delegates from NATO countries and is in effect NATO's parliamentary arm. The secretary general of the organisation always chaired the meetings, which were attended by the Strategic Allied Commander Europe, and all the NATO politicians and MPs from the different member countries. It was pretty high-powered. Of course it was a talk-shop, but it did a lot of useful work. By the time we returned from a NAA gathering, we had learned a great deal and were in touch with what was happening in NATO defence, particularly bearing in mind that at that time the Soviet Union was very active.

There was a social side to it too, and we generally took along our wives and had fun. As we were visiting NATO sites, we were all officially parliamentary delegates, and had to wear official identification badges. Mine said 'Earl of Kimberley'. There was the occasion when Janey accompanied me for the first time, which presented a small problem. She wasn't yet the Countess. Which is to say, we weren't married. So I came up with the answer. Her badge proclaimed 'The Lady of Kimberley.' It looked very official, and the foreigners didn't know any different: 'Ja! Ja! die Grafin'. The other parliamentary ladies loved it and were, as Janey puts it, 'Heaven' to her.

On another occasion, Assembly members were invited to Buckingham Palace, and I went along with Janey, to whom I was now safely married. The interesting aspect of this was that, in theory, I shouldn't have been there. For though more than 40 years had passed, the old rule still held—from when my first wife Diana and I divorced—banning me from any contact with the Royal Family. It seems a bit ridiculous now, but it is a matter of protocol. Although I still have contact with certain courtiers who happen to be ex-Grenadier officers.

By the mid 1980s my responsibilities in the Lords had reached a point where I needed some intelligent help with day-to-day events. It came out of the blue in the shape of a most charming, educated young American named Geoffrey Connor, who had been given an internship with the British government to complete his degree in international studies—and was drafted to work with me as my research assistant for the All-Party Defence Group. He worked for me

53 Johnny (right) with Sir Geoffrey Johnson Smith MP at a meeting of the North Atlantic Assembly.

for four months before returning to his university in the States, and was invaluable to me, so much so that I was sorry I couldn't keep him for longer. Sixteen years on, after a period as senior counsel with a major international Texas law firm, he is now assistant secretary of state to the Governor of Texas.

Connor was due to visit London in 2000 and decided to look me up. His initial enquiries indicated to him not only that Kimberley was no longer actively involved in the Lords but had since died, a report, I am happy to say, which was greatly exaggerated. So he wrote to my son and heir, Lord Wodehouse, and was put in contact with me in Wiltshire—and was able to join us for an alfresco lunch here at Hailstone House on a rare day of sunshine.

Conveniently, my collaborator in writing these memoirs was here too, and later Geoffrey recalled to him the day when, aged 21, he approached the Palace of Westminster for the first time. He was, he recalls, intimidated by the grand building and by its still grander staff—and very, very nervous about meeting the Earl of Kimberley. He was, it seems, kind enough to say that he was immediately at ease because I greeted him with 'genuine warmth and friendliness'. I can be forgiven for smiling at his observation that, during his subsequent work with me, 'the Earl had a way of dealing with difficult situations—he never allowed himself to be bogged down with unpleasant detail'. That, one might say, is politics in a nutshell.

Today my interest in military and aviation matters, of which young Connor conveniently had an excellent grasp, remains as strong as ever. Only a few years ago I made a speech at the Atlantic Assembly when I suggested, roughly, that NATO had outlived its purpose in its present form. I believed that it should be enlarged and could possibly be called the International Peace Keeping Organisation, IPKO. Everyone roared with laughter! In 1999 NATO fulfilled this role in Kosovo. What I suggested has exactly happened.

I was a founding member of the House of Lords All-Party Defence Study Group, which was started by the late Lord Shinwell, with the object of being an unpaid public relations arm of the Ministry of Defence. We invited Commons members to join us too, because it brought more kudos to what we were doing. Manny Shinwell had been a conscientious objector in the First World War. But now, an old man, he was supporting our armed forces, and was bitterly critical of the Labour government of the time for not taking proper steps to defend Britain from its enemies. When Manny retired from the group's governing committee, the secretary also retired and I moved into the niche. Manny and I became good friends, though he was in his nineties and I in my sixties.

How much this once fiery left-winger had changed his stance through the years came one day when he told me:

'One of the greatest mistakes I ever made in my life was to nationalise the coal mines.'

Labour MPs of today to whom I tell this don't believe me, but I promise you it's true.

When the nationalisation of shipbuilding was going through Parliament under Harold Wilson's government there was a company called Bristol Channel Ship Repairers, a fiercely independent private company. The last thing it wanted was to be nationalised. Manny made a marvellous speech saying that the government could not nationalise BCSR because the company didn't make ships, it only repaired them. He drew the allusion that to nationalise this enterprise would be rather like walking down Oxford Street, stopping outside one of the big shoe shops and saying:

'Oh, we will nationalise this shop.'

But the shop was not a manufacturer of shoes. It only sold and repaired them.

'What do you call them?', demanded Manny, waving his arms about as if he couldn't remember the right word. With one voice the whole of the Lords roared out:

'Cobblers!'

As every practitioner knows, laughter, especially derisive laughter, is a devastating weapon in politics. Ask Mr Blair as he faces William Hague at Prime Minister's Question Time.

I was secretary of the Defence Study Group for about eight years up to 1992, after which I became president for a period. I didn't want to be chairman, because as secretary I had much more power and could run it and organise it in the way I wanted to. Later I became patron. As secretary, I organised trips to submarines, aerodromes and the Army, so that our people could talk to soldiers, get into a tank or a plane and have the know-how explained. On one occasion I took the group to Belfast where, without earlier warning, I was informed that the Ulster Defence Association had arranged a guard of honour for me to inspect.

I got out of the bus in which we were travelling, holding a half-smoked Havana cigar in my hand. With this clutched firmly between my fingers, and holding my hands behind my back, I carried out the inspection—as smoke seeped out of my clothes, much to the merriment of their watching lordships. I was followed round by a kilted piper, one of whose stockings, I could not help observing, slid gently down as he marched. But I did my best to appear not to have noticed!

What one did notice, with warm approval, was how professional and keen the soldiers were, and how they actually seemed to like working in Northern Ireland, even those on vulnerable outposts on the border. Now Ulster has the Patten plan, which is absolutely disastrous.

Another visit took us to the SAS, who represent all that is best in a British Army which may be small, but is still one of the best trained in the world. At one point, in a practical demonstration not easily to be forgotten, we were ushered into a room where the door through which we had entered closed behind us—and 'disappeared' into the wall, leaving us in an enclosed box. We were told to stand about two feet from each other and not to move. The lights went out and it was complete and utter blackness, not a hint of light. After about five minutes I could hear my own breathing, and the breath of those to each side of me. Nothing else.

Then the lights came on, and standing in front of me was an SAS man with a gun pointed right between my eyes. We hadn't heard the merest sound, yet here were ten rubber-suited soldiers, one standing before each of us, a gun at each of our heads.

It was rather encouraging—as long as they were on our side!

On the wider front, our programme kept us informed of political and military defence matters, including hardware. Then, when a defence debate came up, group members would understand the issues and be able to speak on them. We had no powers, but a lot of influence, because the Ministry of Defence always listened to us, and gave us every support and help.

Until 1993 I was closely involved with House of Lords activities. After that I still attended frequently, made speeches and put down awkward questions, no matter who was in power. Both needed hammering.

* * *

So there we were. I with a rewarding involvement in the Lords and, with Janey, securely married and contentedly at home in Hailstone House, living an agreeable social life of house parties, shoots, fishing expeditions, visitors and dinner parties. All seemed serenely set for the years ahead.

Then, on 29 March 1998, out of the blue came—The Stroke. Remember my family motto? 'Frappe fort—Strike Hard'. The stroke took it literally and hit me like a battering ram. I'm still alive for one good reason—Janey's total refusal to let me die.

TWELVE

THE 1990S

Who's Who lists my recreations as shooting, fishing, gardening and bridge. As we settled comfortably into the 1990s and what I ironically called our 'gentry life', they became, together with visits to Hailstone House of so many good friends, part of the seasonal pattern. Even better, I could share it all with Janey. Though she's never used a gun, she enjoyed being involved in shooting weekends; was a very good angler; shared with me a love of the details of gardening; and became very good at bridge, which I taught her to play. She's also a keen golfer.

Gradually my involvement in the House of Lords eased off, which was probably a good thing considering the changes there brought about by the Blair government in the name of reform. As the Lords was constituted, there was, and is, nothing better on offer to put in its place. I really thought that the reforms would never happen, and that Lord Cranborne, Leader of the Lords at that time, would have been clever enough to deal with Blair and his cronies. But he wasn't.

As usual with the Blair government, who invariably fail to think things through, what emerged was a mishmash. It was like a lot of Daleks swivelling about and shrieking, 'Exterminate. Exterminate'. If only the government would say what they want to do. But they won't, because they don't know. Of course you could fill up the Lords with little Blairs. But if you make it too strong it will end up being stronger than the Commons. At least, we do have the ironical satisfaction of seeing the 'reformed' house, which Blair thought he had tamed, refusing even more firmly than did the old House to toe the Government line.

Years back my old friend Johnny (Duke of) Buccleuch fought and beat the odious Robin Cook in the Edinburgh North constituency, and represented it for thirteen years up to 1973 when he succeeded to the dukedom. When the reform business was at its height, he wrote to either the *Daily Telegraph* or *The Times*, I can't remember which, and pointed out that he was a very democratic peer who had fought and won a parliamentary seat in a general election. But did he not also have a right, he enquired, to be placed in the Lords by God, as opposed to being put there by a temporary prime minister? There could be something in that. The old Lords wholly retained a sense of duty, which is rare in public life today. Whether such a sense will survive in the present House only time will tell.

Talk of reform had been in the air for nigh on two decades, before it actually happened. At least one could escape politics and intrigues by heading up the Great North Road to Scotland for a week's fishing, surrounded by cheerful company. For many seasons I took Kinveachy Lodge, a fishing lodge on the River Spey which belonged to the Earl of Seafield, confident that my favourite gillie would be on hand and that some good sport was certain.

In the Lodge we had some good parties, because not everybody fished—and certain people brought up their 'fishing wives', and left their real wives with the children in Marbella, or wherever. On one of these expeditions I was the butt of a practical joke which, ever since, has never ceased to be retold, and embellished along the way.

Who else to tell the story but the eloquent bard of so many of our events and adventures, Fat Man, as we affectionately call him, otherwise Jeremy Churcher?:

> I would drive with Johnny up to Scotland, everything having been planned with military precision. Stopping places for fuel and water were pre-planned. So was a hotel *en route*, though before we arrived the hotel was telephoned to say we would shortly be smoothing up the drive.
>
> It was all very well done, Johnny ever meticulous. You can't fault him, no matter what he is doing.
>
> And so we would arrive at length at Kinveachy, where there were girls who cooked and looked after the place, and did a beautiful job. We all ate together, anything up to 16 of us, round a large table in the dining room. On one particular occasion, we had a honeymoon couple in the party, City man Robin D'Abo and his new wife Judy, whom I had known since she was a youngster of 17 or 18.
>
> One particularly good night, when a lot of booze was being consumed, Johnny said a fairly early good-night to everyone (he was always up and away early after the salmon) and headed off to his room, which was right at the head of the main staircase.
>
> Actually, it was a sort of semi-suite of rooms, which Johnny

always reserved for himself—after all, it was his fishing party. There was a round turret on the outside of the building, which incorporated bathroom and lavatory, and the bedroom was the square bit on the edge of the turret.

Johnny marched upstairs, into his suite, and closed the door behind him. At which Robin D'Abo whispered urgently:

'Right, get to work'.

He produced one of those full-sized rubber dolls of a nubile woman. Everyone had had quite a lot to drink, certain people who shall remain nameless had had an awful lot to drink. We huffed and puffed and pulled and finally blew up this bloody doll. I carried it upstairs and Robin hurried us on.

'We've got to get in quick', he said.

We hadn't been able to do all this preparation beforehand because Johnny was always there. Robin now produced a blonde wig, and, while Johnny was in the bathroom, rushed the doll into his bed, put the blonde wig on it, rolled it slightly to one side and pulled up the covers just to her neck, leaving a bit of cleavage. Then we were out and closed the door behind us.

We knew that Johnny never put on the bedroom light. He came out of the bathroom and just climbed into bed—on the side where we had put the doll. We then all listened at the door, a damned great thick Scottish baronial door, but Johnny was only about eight feet away from us and we could hear everything.

Now as it happened, there was one very attractive lady on this trip who was the only blonde. Sheira, the Hon. Lady Brinckman, and her husband Roddy were downstairs in the Lodge, but neither of them knew what was going on upstairs. In the semi-light of his bedroom, however (it was summer time, and it never really got dark) Johnny assumed, knowing there was only one blonde in the lodge, that …

Anyway, what we now heard went something like this:

'Sheira, is that you? Now Sheira … now, if I was a younger man … Sheira, this is very nice, but you know, Roddy is a very dear friend of mine. I really think that you should get out of my bed. Sheira, this is the last time I am going to say this … .'

We were collapsed outside, rolling with laughter, until we suddenly heard a furious 'Waa-g-gh' as Johnny realised the nature of what he was dealing with. He came powering out of the room and we fled in every direction. People were jumping into bed, fully clothed, as Johnny raced round to every door, battering upon them, still clutching a half-inflated doll and yelling:

'Who was it? Who did it?'

There wasn't much sleep that night, except perhaps for those who cried themselves to slumber with helpless laughter.

Of such is salmon fishing. But, expert as Johnny was in this pursuit, I often had to hump him around a bit in the river when the current was running. I have seen him going slowly downstream, and not wanting to. He always had a stick or two, and life jackets and whistles. To all appearances, he was prepared for casting himself into the North Sea on a bad night.

Storytellers, by their very nature, exaggerate mightily.

Another teller of rattling good tales and an old friend of mine had fished around the globe, tackling marlin, warhoos, dolphins, tuna and barracuda. But he had never caught a salmon. So naturally I invited Frederick Forsyth, Freddie to his friends, up to Scotland and Kinveachy. My reward was a piece of epic verse whose artistry will probably outlast *The Day of the Jackal*. Freddie called it:

The Ballad of Johnny K.

Being a lewd dissertation by an anonymous rogue upon the several pleasures to be enjoyed while taking the salmon in company of My Lord of Kimberley at Kinveachy Lodge, Inverness-shire, in the month of May, year of grace 1990.

SUNDAY EVENING

So we boarded the plane
(or the car or the train)
And we sped off to Scotland the Bonny
We'd packed up our rods
(With some odds and some sods)
To be taking the salmon with Johnny.

We arrived rather late
Having shot past the gate
And walked in for the first presentation
They said 'Have a cuppa:

You're too late for supper
But we'll fix you a small cold collation.'

MONDAY FORENOON

On a breakfast of gammon
It's off for the salmon
With gaff, net, waders and flies.
I went in like a hero ...
Jesus ... It's zero ...
My asshole got such a surprise.

Poor Liz (as we feared)
Has just disappeared
For the second time into the river;
Sandy's poorly in bed
And young Henry's gone red,
While John's knocking shit from his liver.

MONDAY AFTERNOON

I'm up to my tush
In half melted slush
And my language is getting much cruder
And I think of the beer
I was drinking last year
Knee deep in the sea of Bermuda.

TUESDAY FORENOON

The men all a-shiver
Are back in the river
The girls in their quarters have tarried.
They've been at it like stoats,
(or rabbits or goats)
And not one of the darlings is married.

I've a frostbitten thumb
And a gangrenous bum;
It must be the effect of cold water
But my poor little dick
Is in terrible nick
And seems to be getting much shorter.

TUESDAY AFTERNOON

The silence was sundered
When in Mad Max thundered
Having driven non-stop through the night.
He ate supper and left
Leaving Roddy bereft
For he'd scoffed every langouste in sight.

WEDNESDAY FORENOON

My casting's a farce
I've just sat on my arse
And these boulders could do with a grader.
My fly's up a tree
And I'm desperate to pee
And a condom's got stuck to my wader.

I'm afraid that young Jillie
S'been pulled off a gillie
To everyone's total surprise.
She swears that the sod
Tried to show her his rod
But got stuck while undoing his flies.

WEDNESDAY AFTERNOON

I'm wet and I'm cold
(if I may make so bold)
And my bollocks are turning to jelly.
The salmon for me
As I now clearly see
Is the one I shall buy from the deli.

WEDNESDAY EVENING

So I trudge off to bed
With a thunderous head
To be greeted by dear little Sandy.
I creep under the cover
She says, 'Hello Lover'
I reply 'For God's sake don't get randy.'

For it's no bloody good
My hands are like wood

And I'm losing my grip in the clinches.
I took too long to sup
So I can't get it up
And my willie has shrunk several inches.

THURSDAY FORENOON

I went back in the river
My nuts all a quiver
And offered a prayer to my maker.
And he granted my wish
For I caught me a fish
Fifteen pounds and a house-record breaker.

My backside is wheezing
My bollocks are freezing
But still prayers of thanks I am giving.
And the deep-frozen piles
Are all wreathed in smiles
To be back in the land of the living.

FRIDAY

So it's hey nonny nonny
And farewell to Johnny
And Janey and Sarah and Co.
For I'm back to the farm
Where I'll come to no harm
And the water ain't liquified snow.

And it's here to the Spey
In the sweet month of May
And to Scotland the brave and the bonny.
For we'd laughter and luck,
Food, drink and a ... kiss?
While taking the salmon with Johnny.

Another guest at Kinveachy from time to time was Max Hastings, the distinguished journalist and broadcaster, and a keen shot and sportsman, though not one open to advice and good counsel. A gentleman, one might say, with a will of his own. Here is another tale (unusually brief for him) from Churcher the Bard:

We had just finished lunch and Johnny gave us all our positions on the different beats of the river. He said to Max:

'Now you get in here, Max. There's a shallow bit there, and a rock'.

'Ye-es', said Max, and waded in.

Everybody with one voice cried:

'Max, not there ... .'

But he didn't listen, went straight on ... and disappeared from view, to rise again from the water, moments later, still clutching his fishing rod. Johnny said to him:

'I did try to warn you'.

'But Max was very cross. I remember he did catch one fish, which we smoked for him. However, he left early, so didn't take it with him. Johnny arranged for the fish to be frozen and wrapped, and I was told off to deliver it to Max at his London club, Brooks's. I went up to town the next day and got as far as the door of Brooks's—I am never dressed for such places, so they wouldn't let me in, naturally.

'Ye-es?' enquired the doorman in a condescending way.

I explained that I had a smoked salmon to deliver to one of his members.

'Who might that be ... , Sir?'

'Well, he is a rather tall, dark, slightly obnoxious fellow.'

'Ah', said the doorman, brightening. 'That will be Mr Hastings.'

Fishing stories like these abound, though one of my favourites is more an anecdote than a tale. A good friend through many years, known to Janey a long time before I made his acquaintance, is Peter McNally, whom I first met at a Liberal ball at the Hilton Hotel. He had been brought there by Lord (Rollo) Denbigh, whom I pulled into the Liberal Party in the Lords.

Peter was a very keen fisherman, and had a bit of fishing on a very good trout stream at Stratfieldsaye, which belonged to the Duke of Wellington. The first time I went there, in about 1985, I had only just started fly fishing. It was a very, very hot day and I'd made a good catch.

There was a very young river keeper, and he was walking up and down the river bank seeing that everything was in order. Suddenly I heard him cry out: 'Jesus Christ!'

I ran to see what was wrong, and discovered that he had come across Janey, who was lying sunbathing by the riverside, stark naked and looking quite beautiful. It has to be admitted that Janey will take her clothes off at the slightest provocation, when it is warm and sunny!

From fishing, it is an easy step for me to shooting. For though I adore the one, I've had a passion for the other right from my boyhood in the park at Kimberley. No sooner had I returned there after the war that I took up the sport again in earnest, hosting my own shooting parties and accepting invitations from friends across the county.

It was about this time that, in the Guards Club in town, I ran into Johnny Neville, a fellow Grenadier in my battalion, and nicknamed the General. He was a very amusing fellow, tall, dark hair, Spanish looking, and a great and successful gambler. Whatever he chose to do, he did it well. He was one of those talented jacks of all trades, and master of several.

We started talking about grouse and shooting, and told me he rented a little grouse moor. I hadn't shot grouse for a very long time, and he suggested I join the next shoot. It was the beginning of a long association, so that in course of time I was able to take Janey with me, plus our dog—a flat-coated retriever, naturally. The moor was above Loch Tay, in spectacular scenery, and we had some wonderful times there.

Through the shooting years, as I think back, three names come to my mind, of men whose friendship I have valued, Lord (Harry) Ashcombe, Felix Fenston and Prince Stanislas Radziwill. Harry and I were best friends as little boys aged between six and eight, in London, in Leicestershire, and at Kimberley, to which he came several times in the late 1930s, when we were youngsters.

Immediately after the war, when I was back at Kimberley from my active service on the Continent, I decided one day to take a ride in the old jeep which I kept up at the big house. I spotted a figure walking with a dog across the park between the hall and the river. I drove across towards him, and found to my astonishment that it was Harry Ashcombe. Like me, he had fought in Europe, he in the Air Force, I in the Grenadiers. I'd heard that when he came home, he'd taken a job in Newmarket as an assistant trainer, and had become a very good amateur jockey.

'Harry, what on earth are you doing here?', I asked.

'I decided I'd had such happy times here before the war that I wanted to come back and see it again', he replied.

There was something very odd about his behaviour. He was then living at Horsham St Faith, on the opposite side of Norwich from Kimberley. After some conversation, I offered to give him a lift back. But he told me he must not be seen in a car—he must arrive in a bus.

I didn't enquire further and off he went. It was years later that I met him again, when Kimberley was long gone and I was shooting on friends' estates. It was thus that our tracks crossed at Helmsley, in Yorkshire, on Lord Feversham's estate, where Harry, Felix and Stash (the diminutive by which we all called Stanislas) and I became frequent guests. I never asked about that puzzling day back in 1945, so never knew the answer to Harry's strange behaviour.

Prince Radziwill (who married Jackie Kennedy Onassis's sister Lee) was a wonderful character who always retained a very strong accent, and was notable for invariably peppering his sentences with the word 'shit', except, of course, that he always pronounced it 'shee-et'.

During one of the Helmsley shoots, he, Felix and I were staying at the local inn, the Black Swan. Felix was at one end of the breakfast table with the *Financial Times*, I was at the other with *The Times*. Stash came down, and Felix asked him:

'Have you taken up that share option?'

The Prince: 'What is thees option?'

'Oh, but you must know. It has to be taken up by 9.30 this morning.'

It was then 9.20 a.m. We explained that the option was in the Swanage Harbour Investment Trust—which did not exist, though we did not tell him that. Stash rushed out of the room to the nearest telephone, and rang his broker. We promptly left the breakfast table and headed hotfoot for the shoot. It was there, some time later, that Stash caught up with us. He advanced gloweringly towards us and growled:

'You bloody shee-ets.'

But he still hadn't tumbled to what the mythical trust name we'd invented, spelt out—S.H.I.T. After which (but seeing the joke now) he made it clear that we were even bigger shee-ets than he'd realised.

Many years later at Helmsley, when Stash was managing the Feversham estate, he said to me:

'Now you no longer have an estate of your own, you will shoot here with me until the day I die.' And I did.

54 His Serene Highness Prince Stanislas Radziwill ('Stas') (left) with Felix Fenston.

Right at the end of one of his last shoots there, shortly before
Stash's death, the beaters were at the bottom of a hill and everyone
was down there. A pheasant came off the hill at a difficult angle.
Stash raised his gun and shot it cleanly. It was a brilliant shot.

'You will never shoot another pheasant like that', I declared
admiringly.

'True,' responded Stash. 'My shooting gets better but my fucking
gets worse.'

There was a huge roar of laughter from about a hundred people,
beaters, shooters, guests and friends, which rippled through the valley
like an affectionate salute.

Stanislas Radziwill died soon afterwards. He was a very dear man,
and I remember him with fondness.

While I was still attending the Lords, it was convenient to stay
during the week at our Westminster flat, on the fifth floor of a block
called Marsham Court, where Janey would often join me. Then at the
end of the week we'd head back for Wiltshire, leaving early to miss
the traffic on the M4.

On one occasion Jeremy Churcher was staying with us. When the
time came to leave London and get on our way, he and I were sitting
in the car outside Marsham Court, on a single yellow line, immediately in front of the steps of the building. We were, it goes without
saying, waiting for Janey, for whom packing a suitcase is invariably
a complex and time-consuming business. Which is to say, it sometimes took a little bit longer than one would assume. As always when
Jeremy is on hand, he being our undisputed storyteller, I hand over
to him:

> Johnny was getting impatient. We had reached the 3 p.m.
> deadline for getting on the M4. He asked me to go upstairs,
> hurry up Janey and get the bags down.
>
> 'Johnny is getting a bit ratty', I told her. 'It's time to come
> down.'
>
> I descended to the car, but ten minutes later there was still
> no Janey.
>
> 'Go up again', commanded Johnny, 'and this time, take the
> porter with you'.
>
> I left him drumming his fingers on the steering wheel.
> Finally he decided he'd had enough and came up to see what
> was going on. So, the scenario now is that Janey, Johnny, the

55 Prince Stanislas Radziwill.

porter and I are all up on the 5th floor. Below, the car is sitting, unoccupied, outside the building—on a single yellow line.

Even as Johnny was coming up, the porter was bringing Janey's luggage to the lift. One should add at this point that the lift at Marsham court is very small, which means a bit of a squeeze for two people and their bags. So getting us all down, porter included, was going to take a little time.

Imagine his Lordship's reaction when he gets back to his car to find that, speedily and all too efficiently, it has been clamped!

He was able to get it released fairly quickly, though there were black faces, and a strained silence, all the way home.

But that was not to be the end of it. Johnny wrote a letter of complaint, in his own inimitable style, to the Commissioner of Police. Now the reaction for you and me would have been . . .

'Yer, yer, well, bollocks to you, mate'.

But for the Rt. Hon. the Earl of Kimberley, from the hand of the Commissioner of Police himself, it was:

'Oh, do come to lunch with the Assistant Commissioner and myself and we will talk about this.'

And when Johnny arrives for the luncheon, and settles down at table, it is …

'Now, don't worry about a thing, Lord Kimberley. We have
taken care of the fines etcetera.'

To which Johnny responds:

'No, I was clamped. I will pay my fines like any other
citizen.'

It was a slap-up lunch, they really did make an effort. But of
course the whole reason for it, which to me is typically the
bloody Metropolitan Police, at that time and may be still, was
when they said:

'Would you like to make a speech in the House of Lords for
us, on the police and on the fact that the force needs more
pay?'

Jerry's story is impeccable up to the last couple of paragraphs. I
was and am pro-police and the impossible job they have to do. My
policy in the Lords was always that I would help people if I could,
if genuinely I felt there was a need. In the case of the Met, there was
such a need, and I did subsequently make a speech on their behalf.

While the social and country life, and the Lords, proceeded
merrily, there was also a business life to look after, not least the
affairs of my Cornwall estate at Falmouth (looked after for me by the
admirable Mark Bennett), which was and remains my financial
salvation. About ten years ago we sold a bit of Falmouth to Peter de
Savary. He was one of the biggest entrepreneurs and developers of
the 1980s, who had a particular taste for Cornwall. Apart from his
interests in Falmouth, he also bought land at Land's End and John
o'Groats.

This larger than life character was the last individual to put
together an Americas Cup Challenge, a catamaran which was built at
Falmouth—and fell apart at sea. Eventually his business empire fell
apart too, and he lost everything. But while the de Savary pennant
was still flying briskly, he paid £14,000 for the harbour which was,
one has to say, falling into the sea. The papers ran a story that he'd
paid £1.5 million, which was later explained by the fact that he'd told
his bankers he'd paid far more than he really had done. As it
happened I'd missed the story—until I walked into the bar of the
Lords to a cry from my fellow peers of 'Drinks on you, Johnny'.

Many years ago, my family gave a lot of money to build the Town
Hall, the biggest building in Falmouth. But there was a caveat that,
if it stopped being used as a Town Hall, it would be handed back to

us. That finally happened, and this property too we sold to de Savary. Eventually he set in motion a seven-acre development fronting on to the old harbour, which resulted in a bit of a bust-up between him and me, which I lost! I claimed he had annexed a strip of land which belonged rightly to my Falmouth estate, and was not his to develop. In the end, he was able to prove title and we decided not to push the matter.

I wasn't alone in opposing the project. The people of Falmouth held a lively public meeting which demanded a referendum on the scheme. The local paper, the *Falmouth Packet*, held its own poll, which resulted in a massive 7 to 1 against. A businessman in the town even wrote to Prince Charles, as Duke of Cornwall, to ask for his help in putting a stop to de Savary's plans.

An operator who crossed my path, from a very different cast than that of Peter de Savary, was Roger Levitt. He ran a company called the Levitt Group, of which I became a non-executive director. It was, I think, Freddie Forsyth who christened him the Ferret, because of his 'devilish moustache and feral eyes', a name which later, when Levitt crashed, the press would take up in full cry. Although he looked Asiatic in his photographs, in fact he was very Jewish in his looks, and a practising Jew too. He married a Jewish girl who was very pretty—except that she used to round off her red lipstick with a black and very unbecoming line.

Among his other failings, Levitt was a megalomaniac. On the first Monday of every month we used to have a meeting of all the executives, which I also attended, when Levitt would come in and give us a rundown on what had been happening during the last month, and tell us where we were going in the next. When he walked into the room, where about 30 of us were gathered round a large table, we all had to say, in a very loud voice, 'Good morning'. If we just mumbled the greeting he would put his hand to his ear and say, 'I can't hear you'. Once we'd shouted 'Good morning, Mr Levitt', at sufficient decibel level, the meeting could proceed.

One of the men I introduced to Levitt was Robin D'Abo, who used to be in the City—we met him earlier in the exuberant atmosphere of Kinveachy Lodge, on one of my River Spey fishing weeks. I took him to lunch in Levitt's office, and as a result of what turned out to be a very satisfactory meeting, Robin landed a job working for Levitt, on a worthwhile salary.

His wife, Judy—a very rich lady in her own right—told Robin he mustn't work for the man. Although she'd never met him, she was convinced, just from photographs of the man, that he was a crook. Proof that he was came one winter's morning when a story blew up in a national newspaper. Robin and I were both away on a shooting trip, and someone brought the newspaper article to our attention.

Levitt's enterprises, it told us, had gone belly up for something like £50 million. As it became clear later, he had taken about 18,000 investors with him, many of them losing their life savings. Robin was 50, had worked in the City and so should have known better, but he'd put in a lot of his own money. Sadly, like the rest of the 18,000, he lost the lot.

Among celebrated names who were taken to the cleaners was Freddie Forsyth. Even Levitt's own father was conned by his son. Ben Levitt, who once held the franchise for Yves St Laurent, had his £750,000 investment wiped out when the Levitt Group crashed. Levitt was dragged through the courts but, astoundingly, on a plea of having 'no knowledge', he got away with what Nigel Dempster, in his *Daily Mail* column, described as 'a ludicrously lenient sentence of 180 hours' community service, after originally facing fraud charges involving £50 million'.

A brief digression at this point, prompted by my mention of Nigel Dempster! Back in the 1960s, when I was running my up-market public relations firm in London, I gave Nigel his first job, and we have remained in friendly contact ever since. More to the point, in a kind of way he set this book of mine in motion. He wrote a story in his column about my quest for a collaborator to help me pen my memoirs. Through that, I met Charles Roberts (who just happens to live a few miles across the fields in Norfolk from Kimberley Hall) in August 1999 and a year later this book was completed.

But to return to Roger Levitt. He had pleaded guilty to one technical charge of 'dishonestly and fraudulently' misleading the City watchdog, Fimbra. But 21 other charges, including false accounting, forgery and obtaining property and services by deception, were not proceeded with.

I was livid about the case, and pressed at the highest level for the Serious Fraud Office to take action with the greater charges, which carried a custodial sentence. The Attorney-General, Sir Nicholas Lyell, responded to my questions in Parliament, pointed out 'the seriousness which Parliament has attached to fraudulent trading' and added that it was an offence which, where appropriate, carried 'a maximum punishment of seven years' imprisonment'. But nothing came of it and the Ferret wriggled free, even when the matter came up in Parliament a second time, disclosing a mass of incompetence, to the deep embarrassment of certain high flyers. The *Daily Mail* reported that 'Serious Fraud Office chief George Staple's job was on the line last night after he apologised for a catalogue of mistakes which let a multi-million pound fraudster escape a jail sentence'. Ironically, months earlier, the *Express* had reported that 'Soft Option Service Orders for criminals are to be toughened up by the government.'

Pause for derisive laughter!

Lateral thinking, or serendipity if you like, takes me back to another instance of irony, red faces and law breaking. My Mitsubishi Shogun was stolen in Cirencester, and just one hour later the police recovered it, and arrested and charged a youth with theft. In due course he appeared in court in Cheltenham—well, almost.

I received a letter from Gloucestershire Constabulary, informing me that the youth escaped from the court, while under the supervision of Reliance Security Guards—and when he was recaptured, he would be dealt with for this and other charges. To be fair, the police fielded him again a few days later. The irony came in that, at that time, I who had failed to leave my car properly protected, was chairman of J&P Security Services, Mayfair, run by my third son Henry Wodehouse, who is a former Special Branch officer, and Charles Johnstone, who is ex-SAS.

Another business interest of mine was in an airship company. I've already indicated my strong lifelong enthusiasm for aviation matters, so when back in the 1970s Lord (Ian) Winterbottom, then defence spokesman in the Lords for the Labour government, introduced me to a man involved in airship development, Major Malcolm Wren, I was instantly attracted. Malcolm had an idea of making a circular airship which he called a thermo-skyship. I tried to get the Ministry of Defence interested, but without success.

Then along came a Scotsman named Andrew Miller, a bit of a financial wizard, who became chairman of Airship Industries, of which I was appointed a director. The company's headquarters was moved to the Isle of Man, but we had a lease on one of the airship houses at Cardington which before the war used to house the R101, which crashed tragically in France on its maiden flight.

Andrew Miller produced an airship—not a dirigible, which has girders inside the skin. It was round, with no struts in it, but it flew and it worked. Malcolm Wren was furious, and accused Miller of stealing his idea, which in fact he hadn't done at all. Subsequently, three or four of the craft were built, costing about £1 million each. I think Miller somehow got connected to Alan Bond, who had made a fortune in Perth, in Australia, and who became famous overnight for paying several million pounds for Van Gogh's celebrated painting, *The Sunflowers*. Bond put in as chairman of Airship Industries a delightful Australian named Alan Birchmore, who did a brilliant job and really got the company going. Then, fatefully, Bond had a row with Lonrho and Tiny Rowlands which destroyed him and his fortune, and with it the airship project. I, like many others, lost my job and, on this side of the Atlantic at least, the airship sank out of sight.

Within the last decade, and even while our project was still operational, the US Navy has shown an interest in having an airborne early warning platform, and the airship is the obvious answer. It can stay aloft for days, doesn't reflect radar, and therefore is unlikely to be shot down—if you can't see it, you can't find it. It could also carry anti-missile missiles. The idea is still being developed by Westinghouse in America.

* * *

The sands of the 1990s continued to run smoothly and agreeably. I served as patron of the Cricklade Agricultural Society, which runs a very good annual show to which I gave a cup for champion goat (horses, cows etc. were already spoken for). For a time I was chairman of the North Swindon Conservative Association.

Regularly I wended my way down to the Red Lion in the village, to gossip over the bar with the friendly landlord, who used to work on Concorde. I called the pub 'The CIA' (Cricklade Intelligence Agency), because I picked up all my information there. But, unforeseen and unanticipated then, my own Ides of March were creeping up on me, though with hindsight there were indications that it was on its way. I refer to the night of 29 March 1998, when the stroke came which stopped me in my tracks for months, and still, more than three years on, has me confined to a wheelchair. Though my brain still works, thank God, and I'm a lucky guy and the first to admit it.

As Janey was abroad in Budapest, I went out to dinner with two friends in Cirencester, and played bridge afterwards. Before I'd left home, I'd set up the video to record a brilliant Tim Henman tennis match against a Cuban, Marcellos Rios. I came back, opened a bottle of wine, sat down to watch the match and turned the tape on. It was one of the best matches I've ever seen.

I went upstairs to bed, used the bathroom and loo, and suddenly realised that something was badly wrong. Then my legs gave way and I couldn't walk. I crawled into the bedroom on my hands and knees. I managed to reach the telephone and to call my doctor, and told him I thought I was having a heart attack.

I had staff living in, but they were in a separate flat, and I couldn't make them hear me. I rang my neighbours next door, David and Jan Whilley, told them what was happening, and they managed to wake the staff, who unlocked the front door to await the doctor's arrival.

When the ambulance arrived, Jan willingly agreed to travel with me in the ambulance, as I didn't want to be alone. They took me to the Princess Margaret Hospital in Swindon and put me in intensive care. I remember starting off in the ambulance, and that I asked them to switch the sound on, the klaxon. I thought it would be a bit of fun! I don't remember reaching the hospital. In fact I don't remember much of the period that followed, except that in time Janey brought me home, and a long, slow battle began to return to something near normality.

But I'm alive, while so many of my friends and peers are falling off their perches. It is distressing, *memento mori*. I often think about death. I have done so for many years. I did have a vision decades ago with my old friend of our St Moritz triumphs, Michael Holliday. When we reached a certain age, we told each other, we would go up in a Gloster Meteor or something like that, and at 40,000 feet turn off the oxygen. No-one would ever know what happened. They wouldn't consider suicide. They'd think it was a fault in the oxygen supply. Pity, I'd never be able to get into an aeroplane now, let alone fly it up to 40,000 feet.

Following the stroke, I was in and out of a coma for weeks, so I must have been fighting for life, rather than the other thing. I don't know whether religious belief comes into this. Perhaps I am like a lot of others, in that I find belief only when I'm frightened. That's the simple truth.

Setting down on these pages the skeins of my life has assuredly had its effect. I look back—and I do regret the course my life has taken. I could have done so much more with it. I've frittered it away, and I'm ashamed to confess it. Yet in the end, I'm not going to apologise for it, because it's me, the way I am, the way the Kimberley genes have come down to me. I said it on the opening page, and I say it on the last—by God I've enjoyed my wayward life, even if I have to repent at leisure.

And so for now, as Janey puts it: Here we are, letting things unroll.

POSTSCRIPT

JANEY'S STORY

I was a child in Africa and daughter of a war-time soldier. My father was a lieutenant-colonel in the 60th Rifles, who after the war took the family to Rhodesia, as it then was. I was about two years old and the first of four girls born to my parents.

When the time came, I was sent to a boarding school, which was a nightmare to me. All I'd known was running around a farm with black people; and then suddenly—whites only! It was a school where anybody who was black ran away when they saw you.

In due course we came back to England, travelling for six weeks on a lovely ship. In no time we'd moved to France, where we had an uncle who owned a château, and we appropriated a wing of it. It was a wonderful place to be, but it didn't last, because my parents' marriage was collapsing. After three years we were back in England, and my mother and father separated. We girls stayed with mummy but my father periodically summoned us all to tea, and he remained a big influence on us. On the other hand, my mother believed in people making their own way in life and making their own mistakes. She was a truly adorable person, but perhaps in my case I could have benefitted from a little more guidance.

In my early twenties I was working in a bar, when a regular customer, an elderly and very kind gentleman, offered me a job in Jamaica. So it was that I found myself in Falmouth, near Montego Bay. Then I met Johnny at a cocktail party. Or more accurately, Johnny marched over to me and exclaimed: 'Who the hell are you? You're so brown'. The attraction, one has to say, was mutual. When he asked me to go and stay with him, I agreed. I remember I went by the local bus and lost my luggage.

Quite soon, Johnny got himself into a knot. He used me to get rid of one woman in his life. But then someone else at his behest was coming out from England—it was one of the models much in the newspapers at that time, Liz Hooley, known as the Hooley Bird.

So Johnny parked me out and she came in. He put me on one plane and Hooley arrived on the next. I can't think why I was so accommodating. Anyway, I went off to see my sister in Freeport, on Grand Bahama Island. Later Johnny found me again, though I can't remember how. And I went back to him, despite the other women and despite his heavy drinking.

Then Johnny left Jamaica, and me, and returned to England. First I heard about his marriage to Gillie. Next a rumour reached me that he had died. I was heart-broken. But if you think a person is dead and at peace, then eventually your mind and system accept it, and that is what I needed.

It was at this time that I decided to head back for England. I'd been working in Antigua on yachts as a cook, taking out charters, and so that was the way I came back to Europe, in a small yacht as a 'galley slave'.

On the way there was a mutiny against the skipper. We reached Portugal and I was unceremoniously dumped. So I hitched all the way back to England, and was thrilled with myself! I did a spot of grape-picking on the way, so it must have been autumn.

At last I arrived home, having accepted by now that Johnny was dead—only to find letters from him awaiting me, one in London with my sister and the other in Gloucestershire with my mother, and they were only weeks old!

I rang him up, as he'd begged me to do in the letters. He told me he was a reformed character and that he no longer drank. So I got myself on the train and went down to Cornwall to see him. I was in a hopeless situation. I had someone else in my life whom I loved, but who didn't love me. I tried not to get involved, but Johnny was so compelling—and I just loved being with him. He became a drug which I couldn't do without and I did get involved—and we've never parted since. That was nearly 25 years ago.

Then he decided he really would get off his bum—and he genuinely was off the drink too! I encouraged him to get involved in the House of Lords, and he travelled up from Cornwall to Westminster frequently for a time. But it was a long haul. So the decision was made to sell up and move nearer to London. We moved into my mother's house, and Johnny attended the Lords regularly.

He did very well, though later the Liberals threw him out of the party for suggesting that Liberals in a forthcoming general election should vote Tory.

I didn't approve of lords, and I'd rather he hadn't been one. I didn't like being in the Chamber of the Lords either. After our marriage, because I was a new countess, I was granted a seat at the State Opening. I wore a borrowed tiara from my sister, belonging to her Scottish husband's family. I wanted to wear white, but wasn't allowed to, because that is what the Royals wear. Then I decided to go in silver—but that wasn't right either. I suppose I'm simply not countess material. (Interjection from Johnny: 'Balls!')

At Hailstone House we didn't live our lives locally. We imported our friends. We are not hunting people, but we went shooting. That is to say, Johnny did the shooting. I have never learned to shoot—I'll help put in the cartridges, but that is as far as I go. But I do love my shooting dogs, my lovely flat-coated retrievers.

Locally I do try to support things. I raised more than £700 for the Kosovo Appeal by organising a scone tea in Cricklade village. The *Daily Mail*, in return for an article from Johnny, paid £1,000 into the appeal, making our total £1,700. We lived here what Johnny calls a quiet gentry life. There was nothing too stressful—except our fights.

Then came Johnny's stroke. He hadn't been at his best for some time—and he was back on the bottle. Life was a bit of a struggle: he wasn't very happy and was slowing up quite drastically. We'd had a very bad fishing trip up in Scotland a year before, and he was not at all well. But I'm ashamed to say that we missed his rising blood pressure, which would have given us a warning of what was coming.

I was in Budapest when it happened. I spoke to him on the phone at the hospital and he sounded fine. He didn't lose consciousness, and initially he was amazing.

I was back in 12 hours and went straight to the hospital, where for two or three days Johnny was in a public ward. It was like being in Calcutta or somewhere in the Third World. The comforting advice from the staff was: 'There's nothing we can do'. I wasn't accepting that. So we did a 24-hour vigil by his bed, trying to keep him comfortable and keep him moving.

Then we got him into the right ward, but he caught pneumonia. Blood pressure was bad. He wasn't really with us. He was back at Kimberley years before. He was also having alcohol withdrawal symptoms. He was there for precisely four weeks, at the end of which the hospital attitude was that he was going to die, whatever they did. I replied: 'Not here, he's not'. I simply didn't want the indignity of him dying in that awful place.

At the same time they were telling me that I must think of somewhere else to take him, because he couldn't stay there any longer. But when I said I would take him home, the response was that I couldn't, because they wouldn't sanction it. 'But you've told us to get out', I flared. 'That is what I want. That is what he wants. So let us go.'

They washed their hands of us completely and withdrew all backing. I got him home and brought in a private nurse who backed me up and said we could do it.

We set up a bed for Johnny at home, downstairs in the drawing room. I thought he might die, quite soon, on getting back. I didn't think that I could do it, that I could keep him going. But I under-valued his capacity to rally. He was just determined to do so. It was his will-power, as well as mine, that kept him alive. It took nearly two months to get him operative again, before we could say he was through the real danger.

A few years earlier our beloved housekeeper, Joyce, had retired and left us. In the meantime we had three successive couples living in, but it never worked. Then Joycie came back, and it was heaven, and everything began to get better.

In a curious way, the stroke was Johnny's saviour—it took him off the bottle and, apart from white wine, he's been off it ever since. During the initial recovery period, we fed him non-alcoholic wine, which he didn't twig for some time, by putting it into ordinary wine bottles. It was rather a hoot.

Throughout the time when he was really ill, and since, the old spirit has never ceased to sparkle. Of course he gets irritable, but his humour can still be absolutely wonderful. The most undignified things happened to him, and still do, and he takes them on the chin so magnificently.

But sometimes things get so tense that I find myself screaming at him like a fishwife, because I get so angry with him. He is so lazy—like refusing to do his physical exercises to help him recover his physical mobility. He should be out of that wheelchair by now. Most definitely he should be walking, so he is there because he wants to be, because it is convenient, because it is comfortable.

When I look at Johnny I see something very fine there that has been misused. It's so obvious, and such a great tragedy.

You can't help looking back at the wasted years. Johnny is a manipulator of people. He is invariably over-enveloping—'I want that!' He completely overpowers you. He is so intelligent but—and one says it again—so wasted.

If he has gone too far, he wins you back with his charm. Yet for

56 Janey Kimberley at home at Hailstone House.

him everyone is in a different compartment, which is firmly sealed. When, before he and I finally came together in Cornwall, he would move on to another woman and another life, everything was jettisoned, cleaned out, as he moved on to the next scene.

Yet still there is that huge talent and great brain, without the energy to keep driving them—that depresses me always. I have incredible energy but no brains in comparison with his. I feel somehow that I should have been able to drive that machine, but I couldn't do it.

As in the poem chosen for the dedication of this book, I too might ask myself, 'What have I done with the garden that was entrusted to me?'

Yet there are no regrets in having spent nearly half of my life with Johnny Kimberley. He has such oodles of charm, wonderful wit, wonderful personality, wonderful stories.

I can say with Piaf, 'Je ne regrette rien'. Nothing, absolutely! I would do it all again—and I'd probably make him fight a bit harder.

APPENDIX

SIR THOMAS DEVITT'S POEM[*]

The Pickenham Shoot, 1951

This is a tale of Norfolk chaps
Plus one or two who should, perhaps,
Have their legs pulled within this rhyme
Because they go there every time.
But if you're shy of caustic wit
Or having your leg pulled a bit,
Don't ramp and roar, or start to curse
For fear of winning something worse;
For just like rubber flipping back,
The bard may land another crack!
If cynicism seems to bite,
Just look on it in kindly light;
And if your name is mentioned here,
It is, because it brings good cheer;
So please remember—everyone—
This rhyme is only writ in fun.

We'll now consider, each in turn,
And see what sort of marks they earn.

First of all, consider Guy,
Who, for his age is still quite spry;
Recognise the expert shot,
Killing as he does the lot;
Be it fur or be it feather,
Going slow, or hell for leather,
Guy will shoot it in the head,
Killing it dead as dead.
Should a fox disturb his game,
Moreton's answer's just the same
As other vermin gets from him;
He suffers from no squeamish whim
That Reynard is a sort of god—
He ups and shoots the little sod!
(Should this strong action need defence,
Let me explain, to those with sense,
Hounds rarely go to Pickenham
But NOT because Guy sickens 'em).

Red-head Irene, Moreton's wife
Leads quite a different sort of life;
With Mrs Beaton as her guide,
Irene runs her house with pride;
And gives us simply gorgeous tuck,
Quite different from the usual muck.
She buys her clothes from Victor
    Stiebel—
That in itself is far from feeble,
Seeing how his new creation
Sets the fashion for the nation.
Her mind is filled with things of course
Appertaining to the horse.
Talks of martingales and cruppers,
Double oxers, bran-mash suppers,
Snaffles, spavins, hocks and withers,
Giving lesser folks the shivers.
Horsey talk gives me the willies;
I know nowt of horse or fillies.
So don't let's speak about the horse
In case we should say something coarse!

In the days of Rosie Dolly
Henry used to be quite jolly
Keeping those around the table
Full of mirth, was Henry able
Now he's apt to look quite vexed
If Guy says Doodie's over-sexed
Of course they're really best of friends,
And nothing either says offends
First and foremost of the Guns,
Martineau takes all the buns—
With his back towards the deive,
Martineau seems half alive;
Seldom fires a second cartridge,
Be it pheasant, duck or partridge.
Typical is Henry's pose,
From his head down to his toes;
One shot fired, with hand in pocket—

[*] See page 47.

194

Overhead the pheasants rocket—
Henry sees his bird retire
From effective range of fire,
One leg dangling, feathers sparse,
Since Henry shot it up the arse!

Meet Henry's wife, the lovely Doodie
Full of pep as Henry's moody;
'Hey! You cads, let's have a snifter;'
Signifies a real scalp-lifter!
Quick as Piers says 'Where you bin?!'
Doodie sinks a double gin.
As best at pushing out the boat
Unanimously wins the vote;
But be this true or be it not
We pull her leg most of the lot

One needs to be a little tight
If, of one's self, one has to write;
It's difficult to see the jokes
About oneself, though other folks
So easily can see the lot
And why it is I'm such a clot!
I know that you will quickly see
Exactly what is queer in me,
So I must now leave 'me' to 'you',
To show 'me' how I have no clue,
And only this, of me, I'll say —
Because I hear it *every* day,
Yelled by Claude, or any gunner,—
'Sir Thomas has another runner!!'

When you have aimed and fired and
    missed,
Just after lunch, when slightly pissed,
Eddie asks you with a look—
'Surely you have read my book
On shooting etiquette and why
You miss so many birds that fly?
If quick you'd learn to shoot, not late,
You'll find the lesson on page eight'.
But hesitate this sage to thank
For you will find page eight quite blank!

For season fifty–fifty-one,
Guy took in another gun;
Reputed safe, entirely steady
(Being the elder son of Eddie)
Some exploits of this son of Keith
Really are beyond belief!
I'll not forget one shot of Ken's—
A pheasant, and two ruddy hens!
He shot the pheasant up the arse

Killing the chickens in the grass,
So 'Sparkle', not to be out done,
Ran in and caught another one!

Jim Cook, more pheasant-like each year,
With knowledge of the rustic seer,
When asked to give his expert view
Says 'Well, I think we've got a few',
Then taps his stick upon the ground,
In case you think his words unsound.

Stephen, sitting on this stick,
Never tempts his birds to pick;
Swears he never saw a bird
Which is clearly quite absurd!
For empty cases lying round
Prove his statement is unsound.

Sir Samuel Roberts, draped in cloaks,
Doesn't shoot like other folks;
He waits until the bird has gone,
Then plugs it up its sit-upon!

In London's streets, or Norfolk airs,
Oliver Wilson always wears
A double-breasted Bond Street suit
And gum-boots like a riding boot.
Pintail, his dog, looks like a muff
With coat that's curly, long and rough;
And, as his dog he hates to pamper,
Pintail travels in a hamper!

Another guest, James Luddington,
Lives at nearby Wallington;
His conversations crude, but neat,
Like—'Ho! you bugger—Pete—Peet!'
Now that his eyesight's getting short,
He shoots the way he didn't ought;
Instead of firing one shot—Ping!
He pulls both barrels off—Ping-Ping!
In spite of this he's not a sap—
He is, in fact, the nicest chap.

Ginger Dusgate, Squire of Fring,
Fairly makes the Welkin ring!
Be it spirit, wine, or beer,
He will drink it, never fear.
Lavender is what he grows—
But peony red his face and nose!

Lord Kimberley, another guest
Can wield his gun among the best;
But you must get him first, 'tis said,

To leave his warm connubial bed;
For after alcoholic soaks,
And super-energetic pokes,
Suffering from *mal-de-tête*,
Lord Kimberley is sometimes late.

The most peculiar, and the worst,
Of shots I've seen is Lord Amherst!
He bows and swoops, and waves his
    gun,
Then bows again, as though for fun;
You'd really think he's going to sing!
And then, at last, he fires the thing
I don't know which is frightened most,
Loader—pheasant—him—or host!!

It's funny how a mind unsavoury
Often gets mixed up with bravery—
Norman Holbrook's laugh is crude,
His stories mostly very rude;
But he has, with his kindly heart,
Made generosity an art;
He'd give away his own V.V.
To help the likes of you or me.
But when he's fishing on the Test,
Norman's really at his best;
He uses means both foul and fair
To lure the fishes from their lair!

There may be none, and yet there may
    be
More annoying men than Swabey.
You would have to search a lot
To find a commoner little clot.
Why does he think one wants to pose
Right before his very nose?
I wonder why he cannot take
A photograph that's not a fake?
Especially when all around
First-class 'action shots' abound?
And does the public want to see
The ugly mugs of you or me?
We know that Carmel's slightly stout,
But what on earth was he about
To make a reference to her bum?
I thought it really very rum
But pardon me, if I offend,
Thinking his lunch-time quip 'the end'.

I'm sorry if I sound so sore,
But nobody annoys me more!

While his wife, the lovely Ann,
Loads quicker for him than a man,
Watch David Wigan 'have a go'
And give the lie to polio.
Thus hadicapped, at birds that jink,
Or birds that swerve, you'd surely think
That infantile paralysis
Would upset his analysis.
In this, of course, you'd be quite wrong,
For be shots close, or be shots long,
With one arm shoots as well as you
Or I can hope to do with two.

David Keigh, the son of Archie,
Stands there looking slightly starchy;
Never known to put a foot wrong
Only knows the most élite throng.
Most polite, and very pleasant,
Often kills a pretty pheasant

Charlie Schwind, another guest
Whose manners are the very best,
Shoots quite well at times, 'tis said,
If his hands have not gone dead.
When asked, 'How do you spell your
    name?'
Charlie answered, 'Just the same
As spelling "Schweppes" without a "p",
But "Wind" instead of "Water", see?!'

The politics, I've heard it said,
Of Stephen Lycett-Green are red,
In spite of being told by Con!
That 'Socialism isn't on'—
But if to Ken Hill you should go,
His hospitality will show,
Whatever coloured flag's unfurled
It takes 'All Sorts' to make a world.

Many other come to shoot—
Charlie Mills, Bob Hoare to boot;
But time prevents me adding more
To this slightly sullied scote.
If you take the caustic view,
Some imputations here are true.
But please realise—a joke's a joke,
When laughing at the other bloke!

INDEX